4.6.19

1 1 FEB 2020

Please return or renew this item
by the last date shown. You may
return items to any East Sussex
Library. You may renew books
by telephone or the internet.

East Sussex
County Council

0345 60 80 195 for renewals
0345 60 80 196 for enquiries

Library and Information Services
eastsussex.gov.uk/libraries

04499937

⊙ Walking Eye App

YOUR FREE EBOOK AVAILABLE THROUGH THE WALKING EYE APP

Your guide now includes a free eBook to your chosen destination, for the same great price as before. Simply download the Walking Eye App from the App Store or Google Play to access your free eBook.

HOW THE WALKING EYE APP WORKS

Through the Walking Eye App, you can purchase a range of eBooks and destination content. However, when you buy this book, you can download the corresponding eBook for free. Just see below in the grey panel where to find your free content and then scan the QR code at the bottom of this page.

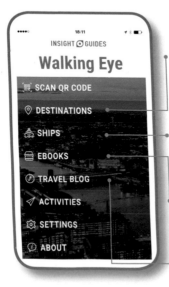

Destinations: Download essential destination content featuring recommended sights and attractions, restaurants, hotels and an A–Z of practical information, all available for purchase.

Ships: Interested in ship reviews? Find independent reviews of river and ocean ships in this section, all available for purchase.

eBooks: You can download your free accompanying digital version of this guide here. You will also find a whole range of other eBooks, all available for purchase.

Free access to travel-related blog articles about different destinations, updated on a daily basis.

HOW THE EBOOKS WORK

The eBooks are provided in EPUB file format. Please note that you will need an eBook reader installed on your device to open the file. Many devices come with this as standard, but you may still need to install one manually from Google Play.

The eBook content is identical to the content in the printed guide.

HOW TO DOWNLOAD THE WALKING EYE APP

1. Download the Walking Eye App from the App Store or Google Play.
2. Open the app and select the scanning function from the main menu.
3. Scan the QR code on this page – you will then be asked a security question to verify ownership of the book.
4. Once this has been verified, you will see your eBook in the purchased ebook section, where you will be able to download it.

Other destination apps and eBooks are available for purchase separately or are free with the purchase of the Insight Guide book.

Contents

Travel Tips

Guernsey's Top 10

The Channel Islands of Guernsey, Herm, Sark and Alderney bask in a temperate climate off the French coast, combining British sensibility with continental sunshine in what is the last remnant of the Duchy of Normandy.

▲ **St Peter Port.** Explore this ancient port with its cobbled streets, colourful harbour and fine seafood restaurants. See page 14.

▲ **German Occupation Museum.** See how the islanders lived during World War II, through recreated domestic scenes, documents, recipes and ration books. See page 45.

▲ **Castle Cornet.** Listen to the roar of the noon-day gun and explore the museums of this medieval castle. See page 19.

▶ **Hauteville House.** Take a tour of Victor Hugo's home in exile and discover that the French author was also an inspired interior decorator. See page 24.

▲ **Sausmarez Manor.** Tour the historic family manor, explore informal gardens and discover more than 200 works of art in the sculpture park. See page 41.

▼ **Herm.** Take a day or half-day trip to this tiny, car-free island and enjoy the walks, beaches and birdlife. See page 72.

▼ **La Seigneurie, Sark.** Enjoy the formal walled garden and exotic shrubbery at La Seigneurie, home of the seigneur of Sark since 1730. See page 88.

▲ **Fort Grey.** Gripping stories of shipwrecks around Guernsey's western shores are the theme of the museum within the fort. See page 47.

▼ **St Anne, Alderney.** An engaging little town with cobbled streets, pastel-painted old houses and a fascinating small museum. See page 96.

▲ **Folk and Costume Museum.** Intriguing displays from rural 18th century life, housed in farm buildings around a central courtyard. See page 66.

White sands of Mouisonniere Beach, Herm.

Overview

Guernsey

Guernsey and its tiny sister islands lie in the Gulf of St Malo and have a distinct Gallic twist. Expect beautiful bays, superb seafood and the sunniest climate in the British Isles.

When French novelist Victor Hugo was exiled in 1851, he thought long and hard about where to make his new home. Since he spoke only French, he wanted to live somewhere where French was understood. He finally chose the Channel Islands because they were 'morsels of France fallen into the sea and gathered up by England'.

If Hugo felt perfectly at home in the Channel Islands, so did the numerous British and Irish army officers and colonial servants who chose to settle here in the 19th century. The addition of new Anglian and Celtic ingredients to the existing French culture resulted in a mix that makes the islands feel reassuringly familiar, yet still exotic.

'Similar but different' is a phrase that could also describe the way that Jersey and Guernsey seek to differentiate themselves from each other. They each issue their own currencies, phonecards and postage stamps, none of which are valid on the mainland.

UNITED KINGDOM

English Channel

Alderney

Guernsey Herm
Sark
**Channel
Islands** Jersey

FRANCE

Letter boxes are different colours (red on Jersey, blue on Guernsey) and each claims its version of the classic knitted fisherman's jumper. Guernsey people rarely refer to Jersey by name: to them, it is 'the other island'. They refer to its inhabitants, only half in jest, as *crapauds* (toads) – because the toad is found on Jersey but not on Guernsey. With their slower pace of life Guernsey people are dismissed as *ânes* (donkeys) by their bigger-island rivals.

LOCATION AND CLIMATE

As a group the islands sit just off the Cherbourg peninsula. With an area of 24 sq miles (62 sq km), and a population of around 63,000, Guernsey is the second biggest of the Channel Islands after Jersey, but the more densely populated. The Bailiwick of Guernsey consists of Guernsey, the islands of Herm, Jethou, Sark and Alderney, and a number of scattered lighthouse rocks and islets, such as Burhou, Ortac and the Casquets. The tiny islands of Herm (20 minutes by ferry from

Walking down Pier Steps in St Peter Port.

Alderney's Mannez Lighthouse beam is visible 23 miles (37km) out to sea.

Guernsey) and Sark (45 minutes) are peaceful retreats, with sandy beaches and dramatic clifftop scenery. Sark's 450-year-old feudal system came to an end in 2008 when the Chief Pleas (legislative body) was reformed, the first general election was held and Sark became Europe's newest democracy. Alderney is the northernmost of the Channel Islands, just 8 miles (13km) from France. It was deliberately depopulated during the war, and used as a forced labour camp. Community life has been successfully rebuilt since the island's liberation in 1945; Alderney is now popular with ornithologists and beach lovers looking for privacy and a peaceful escape from the busy world.

The Channel Islands are mild in winter and sunny in summer, but strong winds can make temperatures feel cool. In the summer months the islands have a daily average of eight hours of sunshine and an average maximum temperature of 68°F (20°C). The At-lantic sea temperatures are cool for swimming, averaging 62.8°F (17.1°C) in summer.

BRITISH LINKS

Although they are not truly British, the Channel Islands have been linked with the British Crown for over 900 years. Self-government was granted to the islands by King John in 1204, as a reward for staying loyal to the English Crown after the rest of Normandy was conquered by King Philippe II of France. Ever since, the islands have pledged allegiance to the English Crown, and as the last remaining territories of the dukes of Normandy, they toast the Queen of England as 'Our Duke of Normandy'. The islands delegate matters of foreign policy and defence to the UK parliament, but in all other affairs – especially in taxation and financial policy – they guard their independence zealously. They are not part of the EU, except for purposes of free trade in goods, and Brexit is unlikely to impact on their historic relationship with the UK.

ECONOMY

Guernsey saw major changes during the late 20th century as the financial services industry took over from agriculture and tourism as the mainstay of the economy. The sector is now completely dominant, generating about 35

Guide to Coloured Boxes

Eating	This guide is dotted
Fact	with coloured boxes providing additional
Green	practical and cultural information to
Kids	make the most of
Shopping	your visit. Here is a guide to the coding
View	system.

Tides

The islands have one of the largest tidal movements in the world; the change between high and low water almost doubles the size of the islands. Powerful tides expose huge areas of rock pools and clean, sandy and rarely crowded beaches. Fishermen forage along the foreshore for the lobsters, mussels, clams and oysters that end up being served as *plateaux de fruits de mer* in the island's many seafood restaurants.

The seawall protects the shoreline and town.

percent of the island's economic output. The almost complete absence of taxes on capital makes the islands very attractive to wealthy incomers, and to the banking community. Traditional activities such as dairy farming and fishing still continue and recent years have seen a surge in small-scale producers such as cheese-makers, organic farmers and specialist pig breeders.

Tourism saw its heyday in the 1950s and 1960s when railway workers flocked over with their free ferry tickets. Today the emphasis is on upmarket short breaks, plus heritage, gastronomy and traditional leisure activities. And Guernsey wants to keep it that way, with no theme parks and no Starbucks.

ENVIRONMENT

The coastal fringes have their own distinctive wildlife, from the puffins and gannets that nest on the offshore islets, to the sea kale, horned poppy and sea holly that grows on the dunes. On Guernsey the island of Lihou and nearby nature reserves have been designated as a Ramsar site (a wetland of international importance). This large intertidal zone has a rich biodiversity of flora and fauna.

Green lanes on Guernsey, called Ruettes Tranquilles, have reduced the speed limit on country lanes to 15mph (24kph) and encourage cyclists and pedestrians. On the other hand, Guernsey has one of the highest car ownership rates in the world, and the amount of traffic and parking problems may deter you from driving.

Cycling is the main form of transport on Sark.

Food and Drink

Guernsey has a thriving gastronomic scene, particularly in St Peter Port. The clear, warm waters around the island produce an abundance of shellfish, including scallops, lobsters and crabs. Eating out is an essential part of life on the island, and with its many wealthy residents, Guernsey has more than its fair share of upmarket restaurants. Even the discerning French come across the Channel to indulge their palates. But at the other end of the scale, there are plenty of humble establishments, from fish and chip cafés and ethnic restaurants to rural pubs offering bar meals and beach kiosks where you can tuck into a crab sandwich.

Freshly caught crab for sale at the fish market in St Peter Port.

FRUITS OF THE SEA

At its best, Guernsey fare draws on locally produced ingredients. Seafood features on virtually every menu. For a full blow out, order a Breton-style *plateau de fruits de mer*, and work your way through a king-size seafood banquet of oysters, scallops, crabs, mussels and lobster. The nicely plump

Cream tea using milk from Guernsey cows in the clotted cream.

chancre crab is the most widely available but the sweeter spider crab is more sought after. The catch of the day is likely to be chalked up on a board. Sea bass, bream, brill, grey mullet, monkfish, turbot, mackerel and sole still inhabit Guernsey waters.

With France a short hop away, it is not surprising that Gallic dishes appear on menus. There are good farmhouse cheeses from Normandy and fresh French baguettes can be bought from bakers in St Port (try, for example, Boulangerie Victor Hugo in Le Pollet). But generally speaking it is British cuisine that prevails. You won't have to go far to find a fry-up breakfast, Sunday roast or scampi and chips.

The national dish is Guernsey Bean Jar, a variation of the French cassoulet. This hearty dish, comprised of various kinds of dried beans, plus pork, onions and herbs, is traditionally cooked overnight in a stone bean jar and served with crusty bread.

Guernsey ormer

If you are on the island between January and April, during spring tides, you may see locals in waterproofs and wellies wading out in search of the ormer shellfish. Related to the abalone, it is found beneath rocks on the island's tidal sandbanks, and has a distinctive shell, well camouflaged from the outside but beautifully irridescent inside with a pearly rainbow sheen. Once a staple of the Channel Islanders' diet, the numbers of molluscs have dwindled and nowadays there are stringent regulations to protect the stocks.

The ormer is sometimes called the abalone or ear-shell.

Market gardening thrives on the islands, but even Guernsey dwellers will bend the knee to the deliciously earthy new potatoes grown by rival Jersey and likely to be found on the menu from March onwards. Tomatoes, celery, courgettes, peppers and most other salad ingredients will be locally grown. Home-grown strawberries will be accompanied, as likely as not, by delicious Guernsey cream. This is sure to find its way into all sorts of dishes, from teatime scones and cream to soups and sauces, along with the bright yellow Guernsey butter that will be spread on a slice of traditional Guernsey *gâche* (fruit loaf, pronounced 'gosh').

Dining hours are the same as those in the UK at lunch time, but evening meals tend to be served earlier, especially at seaside restaurants where last orders are often at 8pm.

LOCAL BREWS

Randalls, established in St Peter Port in 1868, now have a state-of-the-art brewery on St George's Esplanade. Pre-arranged group tours (minimum 12 people) take place on Wednesday and Friday at 6–7.30pm (booking essential: tel: 01481-720 134; www. randallsbrewery.com). Visitors are shown how malted barley, hops, water and yeast are converted into Breda Lager and Patois. The only other brewery on the island is the White Rock microbrewery (www.whiterockbrewery.gg) which produces good quality craft beers with names like Wonky Donkey and Witch Hunter. The billionaire Barclay brothers own 60 acres of newly planted vineyards in Sark and are due to launch a local sparkling wine in 2018.

Find our recommended restaurants at the end of each Tour. Below is a price guide to help you make your choice.

Eating out price guide

Two-course meal for one person, including a glass of wine.
£££ = over £35
££ = £20–35
£ = under £20

View from St Peter Port
across to Castle Cornet.

Tour 1

St Peter Port

Explore Guernsey's endearingly quaint capital on foot, taking in the colourful port, old town and museums. Allow a whole day for this 3.75-mile (6km) walk.

Hugging the slopes that rise steeply back from the sea, St Peter Port creates a spectacular vista as you arrive by sea. Church steeples and steep-roofed granite houses are stacked on the hillside while in the harbour below the forest of boat masts jostle for attention, lending the capital an almost Mediterranean air.

This is the oldest community in the Channel Islands, and it shows. The discovery of a Roman wreck in the harbour in 1985 indicated that this part of Guernsey's coastline was a refuge for seamen even in ancient times. The Town Church existed as early as 1048 and a castle has stood here since 1206, though today's town is made up mainly of finely preserved late Georgian and Regency buildings.

Highlights

- Castle Cornet
- La Vallette Underground Military Museum
- No. 26 Cornet Street
- Hauteville House
- Candie Gardens
- Guernsey Museum

From the 12th to the 16th centuries fishing was the main activity, and St Peter Port was merely a small quayside settlement. It was through privateering that the town grew in size and wealth. In 1778 alone local privateers brought in £343,500 of booty. Wealthy merchants built fine houses and new buildings spread up the slopes around the town and onto the plateau above. The granite houses appear piled on top of one another. The seafront Esplanades are lined by tall and unadorned warehouses, most now converted to shops, pubs and restaurants. The grander houses of 18th-century merchants, on the hilltop above, have also undergone conversion – some of the fine houses along Grange Road and The Queen's Road now belong to wealthy banks and financial organisations, but their conversion has been carried out with sympathy for the original buildings.

THE WATERFRONT

A good place to begin exploring the town is the excellent **Guernsey Information Centre ❶** (tel: 01481-723 552; www.visitguernsey.com; Mon–Fri 9am–5pm, Sat 9am–1pm; also Sat pm and Sun am June–Sept), on North Esplanade, with its informative displays and helpful staff. The centre is housed in a building of 1911 whose grey granite makes it look rather austere – perhaps deliberately so, as this was once Guernsey's administrative centre, where all the departments needed to run the island were based. The information centre sits on land that was reclaimed at the beginning of the 20th century.

The centre organises interesting walks, with accredited guides, some departing from their office in St Peter Port. Themes include 'Ghosts, Graves and Famous Men', 'Smuggling' and 'On the Trail of Victor Hugo'. During

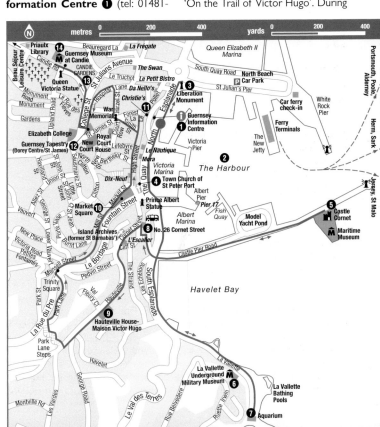

Walking down the Constitution Steps in St Peter Port.

the annual Spring and Autumn Walking Weeks, an extensive programme on the island includes history, flora and fauna.

Originally ships docked right alongside the warehouses that line **Quay-side**. This allowed cargoes of wine, citrus fruits, spices, sugar and wool to be lifted straight from the ship's hold into the tall Dutch-style warehouses, whose large loading doors have been replaced by windows. Most of them are four or five storeys tall, with one set of shops on the lower two floors, entered from Quayside, and another set of shops on the upper floors entered from the High Street. Linking Quayside and the High Street are a number of steep lanes, called *venelles* (Guernsey-French dialect for 'little passages'). Look up as you explore them – some are roofed over using massive timbers from broken-up ships.

THE HARBOUR

On the opposite side of Quayside is the **harbour** ❷, with a mixture of yachts, cargo ships and inter-island ferries. With the advent of the steamship service between Guernsey and England, new facilities were called for; in 1853 the harbour area grew from 4 acres (1.6 hectares) to over 80 acres

The harbour of St Peter Port is still an active port for local fishermen, who provide the freshest catch to local restaurants.

Profiting from piracy

From the late 18th century, St Peter Port prospered from the practice of privateering. This was a form of legal piracy whereby ships were licensed by the British Government to capture enemy vessels and confiscate their cargoes. As England imposed duty on imported luxury goods as a means of funding its wars with France, Spain and the American colonies, Guernsey became a major supplier in the smuggling trade, shipping large quantities of captured brandy, perfume and lace to England.

Guernsey's proximity to France made it an ideal hideaway for pirates.

(32 hectares), with two long break-waters installed 13 years later. Albert Pier and North Pier enclose the Old Harbour, where yachts are moored in the marinas.

The less picturesque St Julian's Pier to the north was added in the 1920s to make way for cargo ships and ferries. Today, high-speed catamarans sail for mainland Britain and France. At the landward end of the pier you're un-likely to miss the Travel Trident booth selling tickets for ferries to Herm, the diminutive car-free island which you can see in the distance. Further along the pier you can purchase tickets for Sark, another popular day trip island, one stop further to the southeast.

LIBERATION PLACE

Close to the Travel Trident booking kiosk, the **Liberation Monument** ❸, a granite 'needle', commemo-rates the liberation of Guernsey from Occupying German forces on 9 May 1945. It was here that crowds of is-landers greeted the British liberators after five years under German rule. On Liberation Day each year, and only on this day, the monument casts a shadow onto the plaques on the adja-cent granite bench, each marking a key event of that jubilant day. The monu-ment is designed so that the tip of the shadow reaches each commemorative plaque at the precise time of the event it commemorates.

The Liberation Monument was designed by Guernsey artist Eric Snell.

A stroll along the breakwater makes for a pleasant evening.

THE TOWN CHURCH

Heading south, you will come to St Peter Port's busiest road junction, overlooked by a **statue of Prince Albert**, erected to commemorate a visit made by Victoria and Albert in 1846. Opposite is the parish church of St Peter Port, or the **Town Church** ❹, whose sturdy steeple rises above the waterfront. Although it incorporates the nave of the town's earlier

The bell tower of Town Church decorated with hanging baskets.

medieval church, much of the original fabric was damaged during the Civil War and the building underwent major restoration in the 19th century. One of the war's ironies was that the town, and the castle that was intended to protect it, were on opposite sides in the conflict. St Peter Port sided with the Parliamentarians, whilst the governor of Guernsey supported the Royalist cause and successfully survived a nine-year siege from his base in Castle Cornet. The Royalists bombarded the town with such success that shipping was forced to move to St Sampson's harbour, further up the coast. Note how close the Albion House Tavern is to the church, almost within touching distance. This is the closest inn to a church in the British Isles.

CASTLE CORNET

Built to protect the settlement in the 13th century, Guernsey's castle was formerly isolated on a rocky islet, and accessible only by boat. A breakwater and bridge were built in the 19th century and today's visitors explore the castle by walking out along the Victorian Castle Pier. (Be sure to get the right pier; from the Esplanade you can be fooled into thinking the castle lies

Looking down on Sutler's Garden at Castle Corne.

at the end of the shorter Albert Pier.) A great breakwater stretches beyond the castle, with a lighthouse at the far end where optimistic anglers cast their lines. A third of the way along the pier you can divert left to **Fish Quay**, where the workaday fishing boats land their catch and gulls swoop down in the hope of tasty morsels. The fruits of the fishermen's labour, including live lobsters, can be seen and bought at Seafresh fishmonger on the pier. Continue along the pier to **Castle Cornet** ❺ (www.museums.gov.gg; Apr–Oct daily 10am–5pm, July–Aug daily 9.30am–5pm, guided tours daily at 10.30am; charge), enjoying fine views of Havelet Bay and the town skyline. Shielding the entrance of St Peter Port harbour, this major monument is a delightful maze of buildings and courtyards, linked by steps and passageways, with little gardens tucked into sheltered corners. The castle was a stronghold of the English Crown for nearly 800 years, and now several buildings within the grounds have been converted into museums. Allow plenty of time if you want to see it all; try and time a visit to coincide with the **noonday gun ceremony**, when two redcoats fire an artillery salute to St Peter Port. Beware the sudden roar!

The oldest part of the castle survives only in fragmentary form – the original keep and most of the medieval buildings were destroyed when the castle magazine was struck by lightning on 29 December 1672, killing the governor's wife and mother, and five other people. Displays show the results of archaeological excavation

Castle entertainment

From Easter to September the Guernsey History in Action Company (www.guernseyhistoryinaction.com) re-enacts stories from Guernsey's past, from Tudor times to the German Occupation. Performances last 20–30 minutes and take place daily, usually just after noon, in the castle grounds. In July and August, the castle is the setting for theatre productions. Look out too for Castle Nights, offering free evenings of music and live entertainment from 6–9pm.

Historical performers provide summer entertainment at the castle.

to recover the form of the original medieval castle, while the present fortress is substantially Tudor in date. It was the first English-built castle to incorporate ideas borrowed from Italy – thicker masonry to absorb cannon fire, as few vertical faces as possible (oblique and rounded faces were better at deflecting cannon balls) and bastions projecting at intervals along the curtain wall to provide gun platforms and protect from a direct attack.

The success of this design was proved during the Civil War siege, when the castle proved all but impregnable, and again when, during World War II, the Germans occupied the castle and found that they had to make very few modifications to fit it for modern warfare.

The castle contains a number of interesting museums. **The Story of Castle Cornet**, housed in the Lower Barracks (opposite the ticket office) traces 700 years of turbulent history. The absorbing **Maritime Museum** in the Upper Barracks building starts with prehistoric trade, when stone axes were bartered for grain and fish, and ends with the modern era of high-

speed catamarans. One section is devoted to *Asterix*, a Gallo-Roman wreck which came to grief in AD286 in the mouth of the harbour. A video tells of its discovery and salvage in 1982. Maritime exhibits include colourful ships' figureheads, privateer licences and Victor Hugo's personal lifebelt and lifejacket – the writer was deeply interested in the question of safety at sea and commissioned his own special safety equipment.

The **201 Squadron RAF Museum** covers 'Guernsey's Own' air heroes. In the 18th-century hospital buildings, the **Royal Guernsey Militia Museum** depicts the tragic story of the death of the Royal Guernsey Light Infantry in spring 1917; and the **Royal Guernsey Light Infantry** tells the story of the regiment, which was formed during World War I and served in France.

A Discovery Pass, available from the Guernsey Information Centre, North Esplanade or at the museums allows 12 months' unlimited entry to Castle Cornet, the Guernsey Museum and Fort Grey, with accompanying children going free.

Cannons defended the walls of Castle Cornet from invaders.

The Underground Military Museum's collection of artefacts.

LA VALLETTE UNDERGROUND MILITARY MUSEUM

Continuing along South Esplanade you will come to the town's main bathing beach, to your left (sandy at low tide), before reaching the green end of St Peter Port, where gardens and trees cloak the steep hill above the under-cliff footpath. Continue along here for a short way and you will soon reach **La Vallette Underground Military Museum** ❻ (www.lavalette. tk; Mar–mid-Nov daily 10am–5pm; charge). The simple concrete-lined opening in the cliff leads into a complex of tunnels built by slave labourers during the Occupation. Whips and rubber truncheons displayed in the museum bring home the brutal nature of the their treatment. The tunnels served as a refuelling station for U-boats, and one of the huge fuel oil storage tanks has survived.

Posters relating to the final difficult months of the war detail arrangements for the evacuation of the islands in 1940, when it was clear that the Germans intended to invade.

Occupation tours

The Channel Islands were the only British territory to fall into German hands during World War II. The islands of Guernsey and Jersey were invaded in June 1940 and turned into fortresses. In May 1945, after five long years, British forces liberated the islands. For information on German Occupation tours, ask at the tourist information office in St Peter Port.

A temporary exhibit of art created during the Occupation.

What was not clear, as the posters show, was whether or not the British government intended to send an evacuation ship to rescue those islanders who wished to leave. In the end, 9,000 people – more than half the islands' population – managed to escape in fishing boats and cargo steamers, including almost the entire population of Alderney. Among all the fascinating military and civilian memorabilia is a display of Red Cross food parcels delivered by the Swedish ship, the *Vega*, towards the end of the war, when the population of the Channel Islands was close to starving. To people used to surviving on a meagre diet of seaweed jelly, bramble-leaf tea and

One of the tunnels at the Underground Military Museum.

parsnip-root coffee, the food parcels, filled with milk, cheese, butter, chocolate, oatmeal and peas, would have come as much-needed relief.

Another exhibit reminds us that most of the islands' fortifications were constructed by forced labour. The people were protected from exploitation, to a degree, by the Hague Convention, which the Germans observed, stating that local people could not be forced to construct works of military character, especially against their own country. Even so, there were reprisals against the civilian population, including the confiscation of radio sets, and executions for acts of so-called espionage. Others were interned in Biberach Camp, in Bavaria, from September 1942 until May 1945, and there are some moving exhibits of Christmas gifts and cards made by the internees and sent back to their families.

VAT-free shopping

In theory, shopping in the Channel Islands ought to be cheap because there is no VAT to pay on purchases and because import duties are low. In reality, the cost of freighting goods to the islands often cancels out the gains. Before purchasing jewellery, cameras and electronic goods you should do your research and have a good idea how much the same item would cost back home.

Boutique shopping on Mansell Street, Old Town.

LA VALLETTE BATHING POOLS

Across the road from La Valette Underground Military Museum, the seafront promenade affords fine views of Castle Cornet and neighbouring islands. At low tide you can spot **La Vallette Bathing Pools**, public swimming pools since Victorian times.

There are 47 displays of marine life at the Guernsey Aquarium.

The first was the Horseshoe, built in 1859 with a small dressing room, then the Ladies and Gents in 1876 and the Children's pool added in 1896. Today all four pools – when they are not submerged by the tides – are open to all free of charge. This is the meeting place of the Guernsey Polar Bears Swim Group, who swim all year round, regardless of the weather.

THE AQUARIUM

The South Esplanade continues a short way to another tunnel: this one was built in 1861, as part of a scheme, never completed, for building a road through to Fermain Bay (see page 34). The Germans constructed several side tunnels, using Russian labourers who left their hammer and sickle symbol on the rocky roof.

Today the tunnels house the **Aquarium** ❼ (tel: 01481-723 301; daily 10am–6pm; charge), displaying examples of the many and varied fish to be found in Guernsey's waters – from perfectly camouflaged baby soles and the tiny inhabitants of tidal pools, to larger conger eels and dogfish. There are also prettily patterned tropical fish, with notes on their habitats and suitability for use in home aquariums, a collection of reptiles in a vivarium and a terrapin island. Fish are fed two or three times a week on squid, beef heart, sand eel and sprats; lizards are treated with fresh fruit and live insects such as crickets and locusts.

THE HIGH TOWN

Returning to Castle Pier, the causeway that leads out to Castle Cornet, climb up the steep lanes on the left that lead right past the Yacht Inn, turn left to the cobbled intersection of four alleys, then right up Coupée Lane. You should come out alongside the **Victorian Shop and Parlour** at **No. 26 Cornet Street** ❽ (Easter–Sept Tue–Sat 10am–4pm, free) a remarkable building that serves as the headquarters of the National Trust of Guernsey. The

An indigenous lobster at the Guernsey Aquarium.

Hauteville House was personally decorated by Victor Hugo.

offices lie behind the well-restored 18th-century shop and parlour, where volunteers in period costume sell gift and souvenirs, as well as sweets, which are measured in pounds and ounces.

Turn left out of the shop, and you will pass, on the right, the former church of St Barnabas, the home of the Island Archives; from the car park there is a superb view over the red-tiled rooftops of Guernsey. Further along, Tower Steps, with its pubs and

Victor Hugo spent 15 years living at Hauteville House.

restaurants, has a pleasing group of late Georgian and Regency buildings and beyond, on the right, lies Pedvin Street, with a long curving terrace of late Georgian houses.

Continue left here into **Hauteville**, where the increasingly large and ornamented houses and villas give some indication of the status and wealth of the people who first settled here when the area began to be developed in the 1780s.

HAUTEVILLE HOUSE

The street's most famous resident was Victor Hugo, the great French romantic poet, writer and politician. In 1856 he bought No. 38, **Hauteville House** ❾ (Thur–Tue 10am–4pm; tel: 01481 721 911; www.victorhugo.gg; guided tours only, Apr–Sep every 20/30 minutes in English, French or German upon request and availability) charge except for gardens) where he lived for 15 years. The house has been preserved as it was and the gardens brought back to their original splendour. Hugo was more than a little eccentric, and the house is a physical manifestation of his quirky ideas about monarchy, history and patriarchy.

Having been thrown out of France, branded as a dangerous radical for his opposition to the *coup d'état* staged by Prince Louis Napoléon in 1851, Hugo first settled in Jersey, where he kept up a tirade against '*Napoléon le petit*' as he styled the French emperor, through his newspaper, *L'Homme*. In the same paper, he criticised Queen Victoria for making a state visit to Paris in 1855. This so angered the people of Jersey that Hugo was expelled once again – this time moving a short distance north to the island of Guernsey. Here he installed his wife ('*Madame, la mère de mes enfants*') and family at Hauteville House, and Juliette Drou-

et, his mistress ('*Madame, mon amie*') at No. 20 Hauteville, which had been his first Guernsey home. This was sufficiently close for Hugo to signal to his mistress from his bedroom window.

Whilst living here he wrote some of his best-selling novels, including *Les Misérables* and *Les Travailleurs de la Mer* (*The Toilers of the Sea*) which is set in and around Guernsey and demonstrates Hugo's intimate knowledge of the island. Growing wealthy for the first time, Hugo indulged his taste for woodworking and interior decoration. Thanks to the anti-Church zeal and anarchy of the Napoleonic period, churches throughout Europe had been gutted of woodwork and paintings, and antiques dealers had huge stocks of Renaissance and medieval carvings for sale.

Hugo bought chests and pews and broke them up to line the walls and ceilings of his rooms, adding his own embellishments, to create a house that is dark, brooding and full of symbolic meaning. Significantly, he chose to write his powerfully romantic novels in a room that was, by contrast with the rest of the house, flooded with light – he constructed a rooftop observatory of glass, with far-reaching views over the blue seas to his beloved France. The family home was an open

Forever French

Despite living in the Channel Islands for 18 years, and feeling at home here, Victor Hugo never learned to speak English. '*When England wants to chat with me, let her learn my language*'. His heart always belonged to France, and one of the reasons he chose the Channel Islands when he was exiled from France was that his native language was understood.

Victor Hugo and family in a group portrait session.

Top of the Tower

For great views over St Peter Port, Sark and Herm, climb up the Victoria Tower built in 1846 in honour of a visit from Queen Victoria, the first reigning monarch to travel to the island. The tower is in Monument Gardens, close to the Guernsey Museum (see page 28), and the key must be collected from (and returned to) the museum

Market Square.

house to many eminent visitors during Hugo's lifetime. Despite its quirkiness, Hauteville House is stately and grand. You can view the building only on a conducted tour, though the eminently knowledgeable guides make this one of the best places you can visit anywhere on the Channel Islands.

The gardens of Hauteville House have been faithfully renovated by the city of Paris, and include a kitchen garden, fruit trees and the oak tree which Hugo planted and which, ahead of his era, he christened 'the oak of the United States of Europe'.

Christies cafe is ideal for breakfast, lunch or dinner.

MARKET SQUARE AND TOWN CENTRE

From Hugo's house, turn left and explore Hauteville, then turn right down Park Lane Steps, just before the Marton Guest House. At the bottom of the stairway turn right to reach leafy Trinity Square. This corner of St Peter Port has a choice of restaurants and, on cobbled and pedestrianised Mansell Street which leads back to the centre of town, a number of shops.

You will emerge at **Market Square** ❿ where the old market is now a 21st-century shopping mall of high street names and local traders. Much of the facade has been preserved and the square is a pleasant spot to sit and watch the world go by. Produce from across the island is brought to the weekly Fresh Friday market, while on Saturdays in summer the square is the venue for open-air concerts and drama.

Even if you aren't a keen shopper, it's worth exploring the maze of the Arcades, to the left as you emerge from Market Street, along with the High Street and its extension, **Le Pollet** ⓫ and Lower Pollet. Many of the shops along these streets have attractive Regency, Victorian and Edwardian shop fronts – and there are plenty of inviting cafés where you can stop for coffee or cakes.

CIVIC ST PETER PORT

At the junction of High Street and Le Pollet, Smith Street leads left and uphill towards the **Royal Court**, centre of island government and administration. Walking up Smith Street, do not miss the lace-like detailing of the ironwork decorating the facade of Marks & Spencer and the estate agent next door.

At the top of the hill, to the left, is the sombre court house, in which the States of Deliberation, which governs the Bailiwick of Guernsey, held its first meetings in 1803. In the same building are the island's courts – civil and criminal. They are located only a short step away from Guernsey's main police station, which occupies the former workhouse, La Maison de Charité. To find it, turn round and go past the little garden at the top of Smith Street, then head straight across, down Hirzel Street. This will bring you to the gates of the former workhouse. On the gatehouse is a plaque showing a pel-

Foodie events

Early July is a good time to try the best of Guernsey's freshly caught seafood, while late autumn is the time for some real bargains, with dozens of eateries offering fixed-price menus from £10. The 'Tennerfest' runs for six weeks from October to mid-November throughout the Channel Islands. Country and farmers' markets sell local produce, such as Guernsey cheeses, home-made cakes, local honey, fish and meat, all year round.

ican pecking her breast to feed her young with her own blood, the traditional symbol of charitable self-sacrifice, and the 1742 date stone.

Turn left here and walk up Hospital Lane to emerge on St Julian's Avenue. To the right is a **War Memorial** to Guernsey and Alderney officers and men killed in the Boer War; to the left, along College Street, is St James, a deconsecrated garrison church providing Guernsey with a versatile venue for concerts, drama, lectures and ex-

The facade of the Royal Court House.

The historic Candie Gardens were established in 1894.

hibitions. Part of the complex is the purpose-built Dorey Centre, housing the **Guernsey Tapestry** ⑫ (www.guernseytapestry.org.gg; early Mar–Oct Mon–Sat 10am–4.30pm, Nov–early March Thur only 11am–4pm; charge). The display comprises 10 separate tapestries, each one representing a century of Guernsey's history. These historically accurate and meticulously worked scenes were created by the 10 Guernsey parishes to mark the new millennium and each one bears the crest of the relevant parish. The stories in the panels are brought to life by an audioguide.

Across the road lies the neo-Gothic bulk of Elizabeth College, founded as a school in 1563, and named after Queen Elizabeth I, but rebuilt in the 1820s using proceeds from a special tax of a shilling on every gallon of spirits sold on the island. Having crossed the road, turn right for the peaceful **Candie Gardens** ⑬ (daily all year until dusk) in Candie Road. Once part of a private estate, the gardens were bequeathed to the islanders in 1871 and turned into a public park. On sunny days locals and visitors stretch out on the lawn and admire the wonderful views over the gardens and harbour. A pretty Victorian bandstand has been converted into an excellent café, where brass bands strike up on summer Sunday afternoons. At the top of the gardens stands a statue of Queen Victoria in full imperial regalia with orb and sceptre. This is diplomatically separated from a more flamboyant statue of her critic, Victor Hugo, which was given to Guernsey by the French Goverment in thanks for the hospitality shown by the island to Hugo during his exile.

GUERNSEY MUSEUM AT CANDIE

The **Guernsey Museum at Candie** ⑭ (www.museums.gov.gg; daily 10am–4pm, Apr–Oct until 5pm; charge) is a

Beau Séjour

Guernsey vies with Jersey for the highest sunshine totals in the British Isles. But rain can be a problem in springtime. This is the time to take the youngsters to the Beau Séjour Leisure Centre (www.beausejour.gg, open daily) on the hilltop above St Peter Port, to enjoy the 25m (82ft) swimming pool or separate learner pool; also tennis and badminton courts, and a crèche with activities for older children.

Beau Séjour offers sports, theatre and musical events.

venue for temporary exhibitions (see website for an ongoing programme throughout the year) but also has a permanent collection of archaeology, history, wildlife and art, some of which is shown on a rotating basis. Exhibits include Rodin's bust of Victor Hugo (1883), wearing a most expressive frown and wild beard, and characterful sketches by Peter de Lièvre (1812–78) of island farmers and fishermen, giving an insight into life on the island in Victorian times. Little ones might prefer the Cabinet of Curiosities in the Discovery room or dressing up in old-fashioned clothes.

Eating out

Da Nello's
Le Pollet; tel: 01481-721 552; www.danello.gg; lunch and dinner. A popular Italian restaurant with an inviting covered courtyard, serving a wide range of traditional pasta, seafood and meat dishes. ££–£££

La Frégate
Les Cotils; tel: 01481-724 624; www.la fregatehotel.com; lunch and dinner. Outstanding, slightly formal restaurant with magical views of the harbour and outer islands. International cuisine using local products wherever possible. Regarded by many as the best food on the island. £££

Le Nautique
Quay Steps; tel: 01481-721 714; www.lenautiquerestaurant.co.uk; closed Sun. One of the top seafood restaurants, with lovely views over the marina – if you are lucky enough to secure a window seat. Chef and owner Günter Botzenhart gives classical dishes a modern twist and his menu is constantly changing to make the most of produce in season. £££

The Old Quarter
15 Mansell Street; tel: 01481-727 268; www.oldquarter.co.uk; closed Sun and lunch on Mon. Good value no-frills food with an Irish twist (Paddy is the genial chef). The early dinner menus at £10 and £12.95 are a bargain. £–££

Le Petit Bistro
56 Le Pollet; tel: 01481-725 055; www.petitbistro.co.uk; closed Sun. Authentic French cuisine in atmospheric and very reasonably priced bistro. Specialities feature *coq au vin*, *coquille St Jacques* and frogs' legs. Excellent-value set lunches and early-bird dinners. The adjoining Le Petit Café is open all day. £–££

Pier 17
Albert Pier; tel: 01481-720 823; www.pier17restaurant.com; closed Sun. One of the island's most popular restaurants with a contemporary setting and great views over the working harbour and Castle Cornet. Book well in advance. ££–£££

RED
61, The Pollet; tel: 01481-700 299; www.red.gg; closed Sat lunch and Sun. A cool grill house and cocktail bar where top quality cuts of beef (Porterhouse and rib on the bone among them) are cooked on a charcoal grill. Non-carnivores are catered for with roast or grilled market fish, and vegetarians with the likes of goat's cheese soufflé and asparagus and morel mushroom risotto. ££–£££

The Swan Inn
St Julian's Avenue; tel: 01481-728969; www.theswaninn.gg, closed Mon and Sun. This welcoming Victorian pub is a favourite for evening drinks and hearty helpings of home-made pies, burgers or beer-battered cod and chips. £

Fables & Festivals

Fairies, witches and superstition reign supreme in Guernsey, where people sometimes still look askance at the water lanes and ancient dolmens that dot the landscape.

According to Guernsey locals, the few remaining water lanes (where a rushing stream tumbles downhill beside the path) are the abode of fairies. Not the butterfly-like creatures that inhabit the pages of Arthur Rackham fairy tales, but Shakespeare's fairies – creatures that delight in wreaking havoc on human lives, turning the milk sour, preventing the cream from turning to butter or tripping the horse as it plods down the lane.

Tales abound on the islands of myth, superstition and strange custom. The prehistoric menhirs and dolmens gave rise to devil worship and witchcraft. In Guernsey witches were said to meet at Le Catioroc, where they rubbed *le verjus au diable* (a hallucinatory cream) on their bodies and shouted across the sea to the small priory of Lihou '*Tcheit d'la Haout, Marie d'Lihaou*' ('Fall from up there, Mary of Lihou'). From 1550–1661 more than 170 Channel Island 'witches' were tried. At a notorious witchcraft trial in 1617 three Guernsey women were accused of killing both islanders and cattle by practising witchcraft. They were tortured to elicit a confession, convicted, tied to a stake, strangled from behind and burnt. Some islanders are still superstitious.

Festival-goers at Le Viaer Marchi honour historical food and dress.

Festivals and events

For full listings go to www.visit guernsey.com/events. All the events are held on Guernsey unless otherwise stated.

Channel Islands Heritage Festival: April to May. Over six weeks of festivities celebrating the Island's past.

Spring Floral festival: late April. Walks, lectures, workshops.

Milk o' Punch Sunday, Alderney: first Sunday in May. Free punch at every pub.

Alderney's Seafood Festival: 10 days in May. The island's gastronomic highlight.

Liberation Day: 9 May. Islanders celebrate the liberation from the German Occupying forces on 9 May 1945.

Le Viaer Marchi: first Monday of July. Re-enactment of a 1900s market fair, with traditional music, dance and costume.

Guernsey International Food Festival: 10 day event in early autumn celebrating the islands' best culinary offerings.

Tennerfest: Oct–mid-November. Restaurant menus on offer from £10.

The islands have a host of annual festivals and events, ranging from local events such as the Torteval Scarecrow Festival to big crowd-pullers such as the August Battle of Flowers where locals compete to win the Prix D'Honneur for the best floral float. Alderney may be associated with grim Occupation-era fortifications, but it has some of the best festivals on the Channel Islands. If you happen to be there on the first Sunday in May, between noon and 2pm, you'll be hailed with a free Milk o' Punch at any of the island's pubs. The punch is made from milk and egg, with a healthy tot of rum and some mystery ingredients. However, the island's biggest draw is Alderney Week, when 3,000 visitors descend on the island for a man-powered flight competition (with competitors launching themselves off the harbour at Braye with their home-made 'planes'); a daft raft race around the bay; duck races and other fun events for all ages.

The view over
Fermain Bay.

Tour 2

St Peter Port to Moulin Huet Bay

Walk along flower-clad cliffs, dip down to beautiful bays and enjoy spectacular sea views. An exhilarating walk of 7.5 miles (12km) which takes five hours, allowing for breathers.

Allow a whole day for this coastal walk, taking a picnic lunch or stopping for freshly caught seafood. Fermain Bay with its café/restaurant makes an ideal place for a break. Parts of the walk are quite steep, particularly as the path climbs up from the bays, but there is nothing that would challenge an averagely fit adult, and the paths are in good condition. Public buses Nos 81 or 91 can provide transport for part of the way. Timetables can be picked up at the Guernsey Information Visitor Centre, at the bus terminus or are available online at www.buses.gg. If you have a car, parking is available at both ends of the walk, at La Vallette and at Mou-

Highlights

- Clarence Battery
- Fermain Bay
- Jerbourg Point
- Petit Port
- Moulin Huet Bay
- Doyle Monument

lin Huet Bay. Although the footpath is well signed and fairly obvious, a map is nevertheless useful. The best map is the Ordnance Survey-style map of the Bailiwick of Guernsey (but not updated since 2010) or alternatively *Perry's Guide to Guernsey* (£7.95), a booklet of road maps showing every little lane, available from the tourist office and shops. Remember to take binoculars for the birdlife, along with suncream, a hat and plenty of water.

ST PETER PORT TO FERMAIN BAY

Start from the South Esplanade in St Peter Port, and follow the roadside footpath past the open-air swimming pools (covered at high tide) and La Vallette Underground Military Museum, as far as the entrance to the Aquarium (see page 23) within the tunnel. Follow the steps up the cliff face to the left of the museum. Catch your breath by admiring the views from **Clarence Battery ❶** whose entrance is found near the top of the path (see box, page 35). This headland is covered in Napoleonic-era fortifications.

From the battery, continue uphill. The path to the left drops down to **Soldier's Bay**, so-called because it was reserved for the soldiers from Fort George who used to come and swim here. Sadly this sheltered shingle and sand beach, which is good for swimming, has become impassable, and there is no public access.

FORT GEORGE

To the right and ahead as you climb the hill are some of the walls of **Fort George ❷**. This massive Georgian fort was built to house Guernsey's main garrison and to take over from Castle Cornet (see page 19) as the island's main stronghold, overlooking the approaches to St Peter Port. It served its purpose throughout the 19th century, then during World War II it became the headquarters of the Luftwaffe radar defences. An obvious target for Allied air raids, the fort was severely damaged in the war. In the 1960s the site was sold to a private developer and the granite walls

The Clarence Battery.

now protect an upmarket housing estate. The fort still retains an imposing gatehouse, with its 1812 date and the name of Sir John Doyle (see Doyle Monument, page 39).

Turn left when you meet the tarmac road called La Corniche to follow the clifftop road for 400yds/ metres, past balconied houses on Guernsey's largest open-market es-

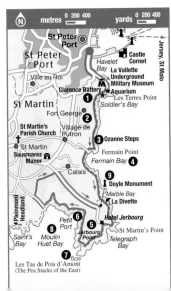

tate – a cross between the south of France and Los Angeles.

Where La Corniche bends to the right, the cliff path continues left, with fine views back to Soldier's Bay. Further fortifications line the path to the right as you climb away from the cliffs through woodland. At the next path junction, go left to descend through woods that are a haze of bluebells in the spring. At the next junction turn left to climb up to the clifftop again. As you follow the cliff path you will pass the 88 **Ozanne Steps 3** which were built by a former governor of Guernsey to provide access to a rock platform where he and his wife could bathe in privacy. Nowadays anyone can come and take a dip here.

FERMAIN BAY

Continue along the path until you come to a junction, then go straight ahead, up the concrete steps, and turn left to follow a tarmac path which rounds the cliffs to give breathtaking views over **Fermain Bay 4**, one of Guernsey's prettiest beaches. Bobbing with boats and washed by gentle waves, the bay has the air of the Mediterranean. This is a lovely spot for sunbathing, swimming in the clear waters (though sand is only exposed at low tide) and diving from the steps. Despite being one of Guernsey's most picturesque spots, the bay is rarely crowded since the only vehicular access is by a private road, closed to all but permit holders, and there is no nearby parking. This does not put off the punters coming by day or evening to the Fermain Beach Café, one of Guernsey's top café/restaurants and an ideal spot for a break. Beyond the café the round tower was one of 15 built along the coast in 1778–9 as defence against French attacks. Twelve of these towers still stand.

If you feel you have walked far enough, you could always head up the valley behind the bay to reach Fort Road and wait for one of the buses that pass at regular intervals. Alternatively, you can walk back to St Peter Port via Fort George Military Cemetery and Belvedere House.

FERMAIN BAY TO JERBOURG POINT

Leaving Fermain Bay by the bridge at the western end, follow signs for St Martin's Point. The path takes you through a forest of Monterey pines and affords fine views of the tiny island of Herm. Shortly after joining a road go left down a 'private drive' which is a right of way to the cliff path.

You can take a diversion down the valley to Marble Bay, named after the quartz found there, or turn immediately right towards the Jerbourg Road. The path takes you just above a seductive and secluded little sandy beach called **La Divette**, with a late medieval jetty. Continue along the

Looking down on Fermain Bay from a coastal pathway.

Twitchers should head for the bird-hide at Jerbourg Point.

heavily indented steep cliffs towards the exposed St Martin's Point.

JERBOURG POINT

A steep stepped climb brings you to the car park on **Jerbourg Point ❺** where you'll also find toilets and a refreshment kiosk. To the left of the car park, the roof of the German Naval Battery Command Bunker provides a good lookout point for views of other Channel Islands. With good visibility you can see Jersey and the coast of France on the horizon, as well as Alderney, Herm and Sark. Closer to, there are fine views of Vau Bêtes lying between St Martin's Point and Jerbourg. This is better known as **Telegraph Bay**, named after an old submarine telephone cable which used to be linked to Jersey.

Follow the road between the hotel and clifftop. Where the road bends to the right, just beyond a granite memorial to Bill Green, look for a path that leads off to the left. This goes down towards a German bunker – one of several along this route, all sited to take advantage of the panoramic views. The second bunker you

Clarence Battery

Dating from 1782, Clarence Battery formed part of Fort George, built to defend St Peter Port from the threat of French invasion. Little remains of the battery but the ramparts have been restored and there are informative panels on the history of the structure. Stunning sea views take in St Peter Port and neighbouring Channel Islands. Nearest is Herm, and on a clear day you should also be able to see Sark and Alderney.

Clarence Battery overlooks the sea, with Herm in the distance.

pass is now used as a **birdwatching hide**, and maintained by the Royal Society for the Protection of Birds. From here you can (with binoculars) watch nesting gulls and shags on the nearby rock stacks, and linnets and whitethroats feeding among the cliff-top vegetation.

TOWARDS PETIT PORT

Continue along the path and eventually you will reach a memorial to Sir Victor Gosselin, in whose memory the nearby land was donated to the island of Guernsey. Straight ahead there are views of Moulin Huet Bay, which you now approach, continuing down the cliff path. Turn left where the cliff path joins a tarmac path, then left again after 20yds/metres, and left again shortly after. Keep taking

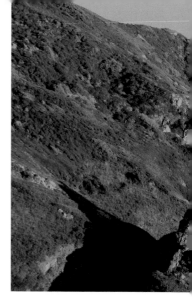

the left turn each time a junction appears, passing several German bunkers. Over to the right you will see the obelisk of the Doyle Monument, which you will reach later, at the end of the walk.

The cliff path next meets a concrete path – turn left here and follow it down to a junction. The path to the left goes down to **Petit Port** ❻ which – if you don't mind the long haul back up 300 steps – is a delightful bay and spot for bathing when the tide rolls out to reveal sand. Our route goes right along the cliff and left at the next junction. The path reaches some steps and comes out onto a tarmac road: go left and downhill to rejoin the cliff path, past a small spring and stream whose waters add lushness to the wooded valley. On the left, the granite wall of **Le Vallon estate** has strategically placed railings, allowing you a view of the ponds and fine gardens beyond the wall.

THE PEA STACKS

As you return to the clifftop, you are greeted by a superb view of the six

Walking down a meandering coastal footpath near Petit Port.

A coastal view of Pea Stacks and Jerbourg Point.

rock formations known as **Les Tas de Pois d'Amont** ❼ (The Pea Stacks of the East). The rocks look like monks, with stooped backs and deep pointed hoods – especially the middle stack, which is known as Le Petit Bonhomme d'Andriou (The Little Good Man Andrew). The story goes that Andriou, a pagan priest, witnessed a ship heading for the rocks in a storm and prayed to his gods to calm the waves. The weather only worsened so he then beseeched the Christian God, vowing to become a Christian if his prayers were answered. The ship was saved, Andriou was baptised and built a chapel on the site. In bygone days

Wildlife

The variety of colour, on clifftop path verges and in wooded valleys, creates a strong visual impact and shows what we have lost elsewhere through excessive use of herbicides. May is especially colourful, with red and white campion, the purples of massed thrift, the woodland bluebells and wild garlic. Don't forget to bring binoculars to spot fulmars, cormorants, shags – and the gannets and puffins that nest on offshore islets. Dolphins, grey seals and basking sharks are also occasionally spotted from the cliff paths.

Bluebells flower each spring in April and May.

South coast cliff path

This delightful stretch of coastline may tempt the energetic to tackle the whole south coast cliff path. It is 15 miles (24km) from St Peter Port all the way to Pleinmont Headland in the west. The path requires a good deal of stamina, especially for the steep climbs up and down from the bays, and it's best to break it up. The walk can be done at any time of year, but the scenery is at its best in spring when wild flowers carpet the cliffs.

Rough steps have been hewn into the cliff.

sailors used to pay their respects as they sailed past Andriou. Today the stacks are a habitat for nesting birds.

MOULIN HUET BAY

The path now passes through holm-oak woodland and eventually emerges at a tarmac road, by a pink and white farmhouse. The path to the left descends to the picturesque **Moulin Huet Bay** ❽ with its striking rock formations. The bay was named after Monsieur Huet who owned a water mill (*moulin*) above the bay. The French Impressionist painter, Pierre-Auguste Renoir, was captivated by the bay's rock pools, cliffs and sea caves: he painted no fewer than 15 pictures of the scenic cove on a painting trip to Guernsey in 1883.

MOULIN HUET WINDMILL

No less scenic is the pretty lane to the right, the original site of the Moulin Huet windmill. If you walk up the lane, you can enjoy the sounds of gurgling water from a stream that is

The view across the bay from the tearoom at Moulin Huet Bay.

Distinctive rock formations can be seen at Moulin Huet Bay.

pump, dated 1828, and a delightful neo-Gothic house whose wooden front doors are carved with wind-blown palm trees.

Turn left by the house to emerge onto a road. Turn right along the road, and left at the next junction. After a short distance you will meet the main Route de Jerbourg road. Turn right here to follow this road south.

THE DOYLE MONUMENT

A short way beyond the pub, climb the mound up to the **Doyle Monument** ❾ for far-reaching views out to the Normandy coast. Named after Sir John Doyle, lieutenant-governor of Guernsey from 1803–16, this soaring granite column is a post-war replacement of the original, which the Germans demolished to prevent its use as a clandestine signal station. It was under Doyle's supervision that the modern road network on Guernsey was established – principally to allow for rapid troop movements at a time

channelled along the right-hand side of the road.

Our route back lies up the even prettier **water lane** that leads off from the right-hand side of the car park, with another gurgling stream running in a stone-lined channel to the left. The path climbs steeply and narrows until there is just room to pass between steep, moss-covered banks (according to Guernsey folk legends, lanes like this are the abode of fairies).

All too soon the path ends at a granite shelter that protects the spring. Alongside is a fine group of 17th-century farmhouses, one with a good example of a five-stone Guernsey arch over the front door. Here you should turn right to take the narrow path signposted Route Fainel, which passes between the farms. The lane emerges at a pretty **parish**

French spice

On a clear day you can see the French coast from Jerbourg Point. Geographically the Channel Islands belong naturally to France rather than to England and, not surprisingly, they have a heady mix of French and British cultures. The great French Impressionist, Pierre-Auguste Renoir, who appraised Guernsey's light with a painter's eye at Moulin Huet Bay, noticed how 'the Anglo-Saxon miss sheds her prudery when she arrives in Guernsey'. Victor Hugo, for his part, was prepared to broaden her mind still further: ignoring Anglo-Saxon decencies altogether, he lived on the island with both wife and mistress (see page 24).

Doyle Monument.

of continuing hostilities from France. Doyle also directed the building of Fort George, and was responsible for three Martello towers – Fort Grey, Fort Saumarez and Fort Hommet, which were built after a number of smaller towers erected more than 20 years earlier were deemed too small. The peninsula here had been fortified long before Doyle's arrival on the scene. You can still make out the three parallel lines of ramparts and trenches running to the cliff edge to either side of the monument. These were originally thought to be Roman but are in fact part of an even older Iron Age fortification. The stone-walling west of the monument is the only remnant of the Château de Jerbourg, a medieval castle mentioned in ancient documents.

Eating out

Fermain Bay
Fermain Beach Café
Tel: 01481-238 636; opening times prone to change so telephone in advance – normally Mar–Oct daily lunch, sometimes dinner too in high season.
This seafood café-cum-bistro is a great place to refuel after a bracing walk along the coast. Choose from crab sandwiches, scallops, seabass or surf and turf, and enjoy the views of this lovely bay. The secluded location entails a steepish walk down the hill – but it is well worth it. £–££

Valley Restaurant
Fermain Valley Hotel, St Peter Port; tel: 0800-316 0314; www.fermain valley.com; daily for breakfast, lunch, tea and dinner.
Contemporary brasserie in a swishly modernised hotel with fine views from tiered terraces down to Fermain Bay. Options include lunch or dinner at the sea-view Ocean, cocktails and steak at the contemporary Rock Garden Steakhouse, or tea and cakes on the terrace in the Valley Tea Rooms. ££–£££

Jerbourg
The Auberge
Jerbourg Road, St Martins; tel: 01481-238 485; www.theauberge.gg; closed Sun dinner.
Consistently excellent food in a modern, minimalistic setting opening on to a terrace with stunning views of the neighbouring islands. Award-winning head Chef Daniel Green, who trained at Harrods, draws inspiration from locally sourced produce. Expect delicacies such as deep-fried chancre crab bonbons or pan-seared foie gras, followed perhaps by Asian-spiced monkfish, lobster and chips. ££–£££

Sausmarez Manor.

Tour 3

Southern Guernsey

A fine old manor house, historic museums and enticing bays with sparkling water make up this 26-mile (42km) day tour of southern Guernsey.

To explore southern Guernsey, leave St Peter Port along the South Esplanade, passing Castle Cornet, then bear right to follow the main road uphill. The road twists up a delightful wooded valley to emerge on the grassy common that fronts the entrance to Fort George, the massive garrison that was built to protect St Peter Port at the turn of the 18th century. Turn left to follow Fort Road, and you will pass the Fermain Valley Hotel en route to the delightful Fermain Bay (see page 34).

SAUSMAREZ MANOR

A little further along the main road, surrounded by gardens, lies **Sausmarez Manor ❶** (daily 10am–5pm, www.sausmarezmanor.co.uk, grounds

Highlights

- Sausmarez Manor
- Moulin Huet Bay
- Gran'mère de Chimquière
- Petit Bôt Bay
- German Occupation Museum
- Fort Grey

free apart from the Subtropical Gardens and Art Park). Take a tour of the house (June–Sept Mon–Thur 10.30am, 11.30am and 2.30pm, first half Apr and second half of Oct Mon–Thur 11am, late Apr, May and first half of Oct Mon–Thur 10.30am and 11.30am; charge) and you will discover that this is the stronghold of one of Guernsey's oldest families: the de Sausmarez family have lived here since

The Sausmarez sculpture park offers a great variety of works.

1254, and a fine series of family portraits hangs in the imposing grey granite house, which dates from 1714. The family has been one of Guernsey's most distinguished dynasties for centuries, having served as bailiffs, governors, naval officers and diplomats. The refreshing lack of austerity is due to the fact that the manor is still lived in. You may well come across the seigneur, Peter de Sausmarez, chatting to visitors. He also takes the Ghost Tours on Thursday evenings.

Only a fragment of the ancient building, in the form of an outhouse containing stonework, dates from the mid-13th century. Since then the manor house has been added to many times. Its most distinguishing feature is the Queen Anne facade, which was erected between 1714 and 1718, and replaced an earlier Tudor building. It was a refusal on the part of Sir Havilland de Sausmarez to modernise that saved much of this heritage from the Nazis. In 1940 the Germans were intending to use Sausmarez Manor as a hospital but decided not to go ahead

with their plans because the house did not yet have electric lighting.

MANOR GARDENS

Delightfully informal gardens surround the house, where you might possibly trip over free-range ducks and hens scrabbling for food in the undergrowth as you explore the lake and extensive woodlands. Unusually, overall admission is free, you just pay for the individual attractions. These include a nine-hole testing **pitch-and-putt course** (Apr–Dec daily 10am–5pm; equipment free with a deposit); the **Coppersmiths' Workshop** in the Tudor Barn where the craftsman is the only surviving coppersmith to make the Guernsey milk cans, used for centuries; **ride-on 7.25-gauge trains** for children in the garden; a gift shop and a tearoom in the old vinery by the lakeside; and Le Petit Monde outlet with local products, souvenirs and ethically sourced home furnishings. Whether you're into art or not, don't miss **Art Park**, one of the largest and most varied sculpture parks in Britain, set amid subtropical woodland. Showing around 220 works by 90 artists, this is a fascinating collection, from life-size figures to flying frogs, with a surprise round every corner. All of the exhibits are for sale,

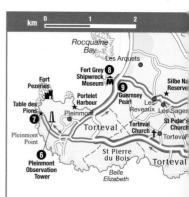

Guernsey gâche

Guernsey gâche (pronounced 'gosh') is one of the tastiest sweets of the Channel Islands, and consists of flour, butter, eggs, candied peel, sultanas, milk and sugar. Guernsey gâche in Jersey tastes different from Guernsey gâche in Guernsey. This is because each island jealously protects the purity of its own distinctive breed of cattle, which means that the milk of each island tastes slightly different.

Guernsey gâche tastes best with a thick dollop of Guernsey butter.

and have their prices alongside – but deep pockets are definitely required.

If you happen to be at Sausmarez Manor on a Saturday you're in for a treat. The **Farmers' Market** is held in the grounds from 9am–12.45pm and has a wonderful range of local produce: chancre and spider crabs, local beef and pork, free-range eggs, cheeses, Guernsey *gâche* and home-made cakes and pies. You will also find handmade arts and crafts, bric-a-brac, jewellery, antiques and plants.

From Sausmarez Manor turn right onto the main road, then straight on following the signs for Moulin Huet Bay. A left turn at the Bella Luce Hotel will take you down a pretty green lane

from where there is a pleasant walk down to **Moulin Huet Bay** ❷ with its sea caves and a waterfall. The bay is best enjoyed when the water is at half-tide or below, as the loveliest bits are covered by water at high tide. This is a gorgeous landscape that inspired the paintings of Pierre-August Renoir.

LA GRAN'MÈRE DE CHIMQUIÈRE

Return to the main road, which brings you to **St Martin's Village**, with a cluster of shops and banks. It is worth finding a parking space in the centre and walking up the lane that leads northwards to visit St Martin's parish church and pay your respects to the

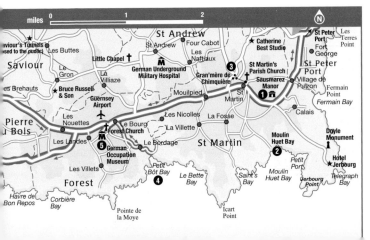

Gran'mère de Chimquière ❸.
This Grandma is considerably older
than most and, though stony faced, she
nevertheless flaunts her naked breasts.
She is, in fact, a 4,500-year-old goddess
carved in granite, standing at the entrance to St Martin's churchyard and,
if you visit after a wedding, she is quite
likely to be wearing a garland of flowers: newlyweds traditionally place flowers on her head for luck. Grandma was
carved at two separate stages: around
2,500bc the block of granite was erected here, dressed and smoothed to create a female figure with breasts, folded
arms and a girdle. During late Roman
times, around ad200 or 300, the facial
features were recarved, and Grandma
was given a set of curls and a short
buttoned cape falling around her upper
torso. The crack through the torso is
believed to have been from an attack by
a church warden who was angry about
the worshipping of stone idols.

From St Martin's, follow signs to
the airport along Guernsey's south

Bathers enjoy the warmth of the sun
at Petit Bôt Bay.

coast road. To the left, after a mile
or so, some of the island's most attractive water lanes run down to **Petit Bôt Bay ❹**, a small but popular
bathing spot, especially when the tide
is out, and one of the island's sunniest
and most sheltered bays. To reach it
by car turn left after the Deer Hound

Gran'mère de Chimquière is an ancient pagan goddess.

Inn. A Napoleonic-era tower stands guard over the bay, and what was once an old mill is now occupied by a tearoom. It is here that the best-known water lanes are to be found. The brooks that run down the sides of these lush green lanes used to power two mills, one of which was used for paper-making. The few remaining water lanes give a feel of how Guernsey used to be before the Occupation, when German forces surfaced over most of the streams.

GERMAN OCCUPATION MUSEUM

The next left turn off the main road leads to **Forest Church**, thought to have been built on the site of a dolmen, and then to the **German Occupation Museum** ❺ (Apr–Oct daily 10am–5pm, last admission 4pm; Nov–Mar limited openings; charge) which lies behind the church. This is an absorbing war museum founded in 1966 by Richard Hearne, who was a child during the German Occupation and still oversees the museum. Amongst the general mass of weapons, ration books, uniforms and medals are informers' letters, a horse's gas mask, wartime condoms (German issue), a doll's house made from cardboard boxes and letters from the Controlling Committee of the States of Guernsey giving instructions for the distribution of food during the dark days towards the end of the war when food was desperately short. Surprisingly, cigarettes did not need to be rationed – experiments in growing tobacco on Guernsey proved very successful, ensuring an unlimited supply of locally made cigarettes. Another rarity is a stone painted with a red V (for Victory) sign. Guernsey people showed their defiance by painting such signs wherever they could, until the occupying troops took to painting

Haunted house

At Pleinmont Point, on the dramatic headland, a watchtower and an ex-military post is known as 'Victor Hugo's haunted house', having been immortalised by the writer in his novel of 1866, *Les Travailleurs de la Mer (The Toilers of the Sea)* which is set in Guernsey. The building was last used during World War I as a signalling station, but was then destroyed by the Germans in World War II, and today it lies in a state of ruin.

laurel wreaths underneath to represent German victory.

The museum's reconstruction of a wartime kitchen on Guernsey brings home just how little the islanders, and the occupying troops, had to live on, once the Allied landings in Normandy had cut off vital supply lines from the Continent. Surviving on a diet of bramble-leaf tea, acorn coffee, marrow pudding and potato bread, the only variety in the diet came from the occasional jelly made from carrageen moss (a type of seaweed) served

The German Occupation Museum holds the finest collection of wartime effects in the Channel Islands.

The Table des Pions, linked with fairies, witches and elves in local folklore.

with sugar beet syrup. Street scenes from St Peter Port show hungry locals queuing outside the butcher's for a ration of meat in 1941.

PLEINMONT PENINSULA

To see one of the most striking of these German fortifications, return to the main road and turn left at the junction. After about 3 miles (5km) you will pass **Torteval Church** on the right, with its distinctive round tower and witch's-hat spire. In a mile (1.5km) turn left, and head for the restored **Pleinmont Observation Tower** ❻ (Apr–Oct Sun only 2–5pm, last admission 4.30pm; charge) with a car park nearby. A prominent feature on this windy headland, this is a five-storey concrete tower, pierced by viewing slots. It was from here that German observers controlled Guernsey's coastal artillery, communicating with the gunners by radio.

On the same headland to the north is the **Table des Pions** ❼ also known as 'The Fairy Ring', a grassy mound encircled by a ditch. This spot played a prominent role in a medieval ceremony, the *Chevauchée de St Michel*, when

officers of the feudal court inspected the highways and sea defences to ensure that local landowners were fulfilling their duty to maintain them. The *pions* were the footmen who accompanied the officers and the Table des Pions was the spot where they took a break to enjoy an open-air banquet. The Chevauchée (briefly revived in

A Celtic cross at Torteval Church memorialises war casualties.

1995) was banned in 1837 because the *pions*, following what they claimed as an ancient right to kiss any women whose path they crossed, made free with the governor's wife.

Returning up Guernsey's western coast, there is a sheltered sandy beach at **Portelet Harbour**, lying at the foot of the dramatic south coast cliffs. This quiet cove with a small working harbour is a good spot for a swim if the tide is out. Beyond is a pretty wooded valley, owned by the National Trust of Guernsey.

ROCQUAINE BAY

Rocquaine Bay merges with **L'Erée Bay** at low tide to form one continuous stretch of sand – Guernsey's biggest beach, with safe swimming and rock pools to explore. In late July the beach is the main focus of the Rocquaine Regatta, a full (and free) day and evening of entertainment and wacky events like raft racing.

FORT GREY

At the southern end of the bay you will find **Fort Grey** ❽ (Easter–Oct

Rocquaine Bay has a long sandy beach at low tide.

daily 10am–5pm; www.museums.gov. gg; charge), named after the governor of the day, and built in 1804 as part of Sir John Doyle's grand scheme for defending Guernsey against potential attack from Napoleon's army. With its outer curtain wall and inner tower, the fort is aptly known as the Cup and Saucer. Today the tower is

Guernsey on foot

In the second week of June keen hikers join the 40-mile Itex charity walk (www.itexwalk.gg) around the coast of Guernsey. Participants can expect to complete the course in anything between 11–14 hours. Those who prefer shorter strolls can pick up a free walking map from the Guernsey Information Centre with details of coastal and inland walks plus all the attractions en route. Guernsey and its sister islands boast a rich variety of habitats for wildlife and birdlife; RSPB walks and events are organised throughout the year (www.rspbguernsey.co.uk).

Explore Guernsey on a self-guided or organised walk.

home to Guernsey's excellent **Shipwreck Museum**. The island's western shores, including the notorious Hanois reef, have seen numerous vessels come to grief. The sea surrounding Guernsey was for a long time the cornerstone of two important sea routes: the transatlantic run to the United States and the southerly run from Britain and northern Europe to the Mediterranean. Most disasters occurred in the peak shipping years of the 19th century. Building a lighthouse on the Hanois reef in 1862 reduced the annual toll of shipwrecks, and in 1975 the shipping lane for ocean-going vessels was moved 10 miles (16km) west to avoid further casualties. The lower level of the museum features a whole range of finds from a ship's bell salvaged from the sea to cutlery and a fine candelabra, and coffee pots from *SS Yorouba*, which foundered in 1888.

Visiting youngsters can pick up a free on-loan Discovery Sack, with binoculars, compass and magnifying glass – or dress up as a sailor, pirate or octopus! During summer months, the History in Action Company puts on performances at the fort in which the Militiaman recounts tales of derring-do.

If you're in need of refreshment, cross the road to **Guernsey Pearl** ❾ (Mar–Oct daily 9.30am–5pm) which has a café serving an excellent crab salad and cream teas, with a sea-view terrace. Rather than being locally sourced, the pearls nearly all originate from the Far East, but are made up here; you can watch the art of pearl stringing in the workshop and purchase jewellery from the large showroom.

A GUERNSEY TO WEAR

Next door you can find items handmade by local craftsmen and artists, and traditional hand finished Guernsey knitwear produced on the island by Le Tricoteur. While the word 'jersey' has entered the English language, the stylish Guernsey is far less well known, and the Alderney is a garment whose existence is known only to a few connoisseurs and knitwear historians (except in Australia, where the term is used for football shirts). The Guernsey sweater was originally made for seamen, the tightly knitted stitches producing a hard-wearing garment. By the 19th century the Guernsey had become well known and Nelson adopted it as standard issue for the English navy.

SILBE NATURE RESERVE

Return to St Peter Port by taking the road inland, just north of Guernsey Pearl. Bird-lovers should seek out the **Silbe Nature Reserve** in the Rue du Quanteraine, just to the north of the main road. Though it consists of little more than a group of fields watered by a stream in the Quanteraine

Fort Grey is known to locals as the 'Cup and Saucer', due to its shape.

The hard twist given to the dense wool fibres make the Guernsey sweater (originally made for fishermen) resistant to seaspray.

Valley, it attracts plenty of birds, and is a pleasant spot for a stroll.

The main road brings you to St Peter's Parish Church, which sits on the side of a valley. A church has stood here since 1030, though the building you see today dates from the 14th and 15th centuries.

To return to St Peter Port take a right turn shortly after the church, which will take you past the airport, and back into town.

Eating out

La Barbarie Hotel
Saint's Road, St Martin; tel: 01481-235 217; www.labarbariehotel.com; lunch and dinner.
Charming rural hotel offering creamy crab bisque, pan-roast monkfish in Asian spices, locally-caught lobster or breast of barbary duck. Four-course set dinners change daily. On warm days in summer, lunches are served outside by the pool. ££–£££

Bella Luce Hotel
La Fosse, St Martin's; tel: 01481-238 764; www.bellalucehotel.com; lunch and dinner.
This is a stylish hotel in the peaceful green lanes of St Martin's, where you can come for light bar meals, a leisurely Sunday lunch or gourmet modern European cuisine, three-course dinners. Head chef Sebastian Orzechowski is passionate about local produce and uses local fishermen and artisan food-makers. The Garden Room restaurant opens out onto a lovely walled garden for summer meals. ££

Le Gouffre
Le Gouffre, Forest, tel: 01481-264 121; closed Mon and Sun dinner.
Lovely clifftop café/restaurant serving breakfast, lunch, cream teas and casual evening meals. A perfect spot for clifftop walkers in need of a respite. Peaceful, with sunny terrace, sea views and excellent, freshly prepared fare. ££

Water's Edge
Imperial Hotel, Pleinmont, Torteval; tel: 01481-264 044; www.imperialin guernsey.com; lunch and dinner.
Sea views overlooking Rocquaine Bay towards Fort Grey are the big attraction here. You can come for bar meals, à la carte or table d'hôte dinners, or its renowned Sunday lunch carvery. Seafood such as mussels, scallops, crab and lobster comes straight from the bay. Traditional cream teas and the chef's gâteaux and cheesecakes are served outside in summer. £–£££

Shipwrecks

'To be wrecked on the Casquets is to be cut into ribbons;
to strike on the Ortac is to be crushed into powder...'
From *The Laughing Man* (L'Homme qui Rit) by Victor Hugo.

When Alderney fisherman, Bertie Cosheril, pulled up a heavily encrusted musket with one of his lobster pots in 1984 he had little idea of the significance of his odd catch of the day. Further historical booty was discovered, but it was not until the early 1990s that archaeologists concluded that the items were coming from the wreck of *The Makeshift*, an English warship from the Elizabethan era. Over the years the sunken ship has yielded a treasure trove of artefacts. More than 1,000 items have so far been discovered, many of which have been preserved and are on display at the Alderney Society Museum.

DASHED UPON THE ROCKS

The treacherous rock-strewn coasts and strong currents around the Channel Islands have always posed a hazard for ships. From the earliest seafaring days, two crucial trade routes passed close to Guernsey: from Britain and northern Europe to the Mediterranean and from the English Channel to America. But it was the 19th-century surge in trade that caused the largest number of shipping disasters. In bad weather captains would mistake the Channel Islands for the south coast of England and steer south, intending to head into the middle of the Channel but in fact

The lighthouse on Alderney.

people, a cargo of wine floated ashore. The Guernsey press reported 'amazing scenes of drunkenness, free fights and encounters with the law'.

LIGHTING THE WAY

The first lighthouse began operating on the Casquets in 1724. The lighthouse keeper was court-martialled for negligence in 1744 when the 100-gun warship, HMS *Victory*, disappeared in a storm, along with all 1,000 men on board. However, when divers came upon the wreck in 2008, it was 60 nautical miles from the Casquets. The construction of the Hanois Lighthouse in 1862 aided mariners negotiating the reefs. Today it throws a beam for 23 miles (37km).

The Shipwreck Museum, found within Fort Grey (see page 48), tells the grim story of many of the local shipwrecks and displays their salvaged treasures. The museum could not be in a more appropriate setting: overlooking the graveyard of more than 90 recorded shipwrecks.

The remains of a jar from the collection of the Shipwreck Museum.

aiming straight at the reefs. One of the worst disasters was the wreck of the railway steamer, SS *Stella*, which ran into fog and struck the Casquets in 1898. The boat sank within eight minutes and 105 lives were lost.

A large number of vessels were wrecked on the treacherous rocks of Les Hanois. In 1807 HMS *Boreas* sank with a loss of 127 lives. A cannon salvaged from the frigate was installed at Fort Grey and points to the Hanois reef where she foundered. A wreck with a happier ending was the SS *Briseis*, which struck a reef off Vazon Bay in 1947. The crew landed safely in lifeboats and, to the delight of the local

Walking across the Causeway to Lihou Island.

Tour 4

Central Guernsey

This 13-mile (21km) tour combines culture and coastal nature reserves. Take walking shoes and a picnic if exploring Lihou Island, and swimwear for Venus Pool.

Take St Julian's Avenue out of St Peter Port and up to College Street, passing **St James's** church on the left. The church was built in 1818 and converted to become the island's principal concert and arts venue. It was extended to include new galleries, a café and in the basement, in a special gallery, a tapestry that took four years to make and shows scenes depicting 1,000 years of island life (see page 28).

Ahead lies **Grange Road**, with fine 18th- and early 19th-century villas and terraces, many now converted to banks or guesthouses. The houses of this period on the islands have nearly all retained their ironwork around the garden and steps, unlike mainland Britain, where much architectural

Highlights

- Catherine Best Workshop
- German Underground Military Hospital
- Little Chapel
- Lihou Island
- St Apolline's Chapel

ironwork was removed during World War II and turned into munitions.

Turn left at the next junction and you will see the even grander houses that line **The Queen's Road**. The street was originally known as La Petite Marché, but was renamed when Queen Victoria visited Guernsey in 1846. All the houses are set in spacious park-like gardens, including Government House,

Catherine Best's studio in a converted windmill.

with its sentry boxes at the gate. This was acquired by the States of Guernsey as the residence of the island's governor after World War I.

At the next set of traffic lights, a slight detour will take you to the **Catherine Best Jewellery Workshop and Showroom ❶** (www. catherinebest.com; Mon–Sat 9am–5pm, Sun 10am–4pm). Turn left, fol-

lowing signs to the airport, and straight on at the next junction. The second turning left, shortly after the junction, will bring you to a 19th-century mill, home to the workshop. One of the island's most creative jewellers, Catherine's pieces are often styled from rare, brilliantly coloured gemstones such as tourmaline or tanzanite. Most of the designs are limited editions.

GERMAN UNDERGROUND MILITARY HOSPITAL

Returning to the traffic lights, turn left and continue for just under a mile, until you pass a left turn with a small sign to the **German Underground Military Hospital ❷** (May–Oct daily 10am–noon and 2–4pm, Apr: 2–4pm, Mar and Nov limited opening; charge).

Tucked away down a green rural lane, this is one of the largest complexes in the Channel Islands constructed during the Occupation era. The hospital is a testimony to Hitler's mistaken belief that the Allies would, as a matter of pride, eventually seek to attack and retake the Channel Islands. Hitler entrusted the task of fortifying the islands to Dr Fritz Todt, who had earlier been responsible for planning and building Germany's *autobahn* system. Organisation Todt, as it was known, involved turning the

Martyn Guille Silversmiths

Just beyond the main road, along a leafy path to the left, you'll find Martyn Guille Gold and Silver Workshop (daily 9am–5pm, closed Sun in winter) where you can watch craftsmen at work and browse the showroom. Among the items made here are the famous Guernsey milk cans, Christening cups and bachins. A large range of clocks is also on display.

A range of silver and gold ormer jewellery is made here.

The rusty door and entrance to the German Underground Military Hospital.

Channel Islands into an impregnable fortress, with artillery able to cover a whole sweep of the French coast.

This hospital, along with its counterpart in Jersey, was intended for the treatment of hundreds of German military casualties in the event of an attack. Built underground, the wards and operating theatres were hewn out of solid rock by slave workers from Russia, Poland, Alsace and the Czech Republic, many of whom died as a result of the brutal treatment meted out by the German Occupying Forces.

The tunnels took more than three and a half years to build but were operational for only nine months. The expected Allied invasion never came and the occupying forces surrendered on 9 May 1945. Instead, the space was used principally to store the vast quantities of munitions stockpiled by the Germans.

Nearly all the military medical equipment was removed and as a result the hospital is sombre and cavernous. Unlike its counterpart in Jersey, there are only a handful of displays, and the dim lighting, damp concrete floors and the very emptiness of the place make it a more chilling reminder of Guernsey under the jackboot.

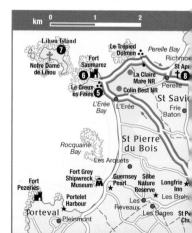

THE LITTLE CHAPEL

From this dank and chilly spot, go back to the main road, follow the sharp bend to the left and then take the first right turn to reach the **Little Chapel ❸** (accessible all year). The building is a complete church in miniature, claimed to be the smallest in the world. The chapel was begun in 1923 by Brother Déodat of the De la Salle Brothers, owners of the adjoining school and estate. The building you see today is the last in a sequence of three. Déodat started work on a smaller first version in 1914 but demolished it immediately after it was built. The second one stood until 1923 and it was in the same year that he started the present chapel. In 1939, when Déodat returned to France due to ill health, the care of the chapel was entrusted to a fellow monk, Brother Cephas, who continued with the decoration until he retired in 1965. The chapel is modelled on the grotto in the Church of Lourdes and encrusted in shells, coloured pebbles and china fragments. Just 16ft (5 metres) in length, it can accommodate a dozen people.

Exiting from the car park, turn right and after about 1.5 miles (2.5km) you will come to another establishment where craftsmen work while you watch. Here the staff of **Bruce Rus-**

The Little Chapel is now cared for by Blanchelande College.

sell & Son Goldsmiths, Silversmiths and Jewellers ❹ (tel: 01481-264 321; Mon–Sat 10am–5pm) make beautiful objects from gold, silver and platinum, including candlesticks, goblets, napkin rings and spoons, caskets and the traditional Guernsey loving cup. The family business has been going strong since 1887. Even if silversmiths are not your scene it's worth a visit for the award-winning 8-acre (3-hectare) gardens, plus coffee and cake or a full meal at the Mint Brasserie and Tea Room (see page 61).

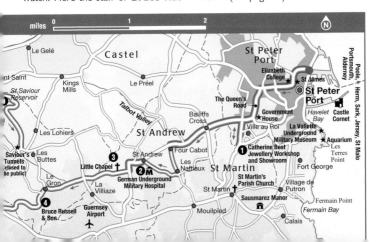

Hedge veg

As you travel around the island you are likely to see a number of 'honesty stalls', unmanned roadside booths selling home-grown fruit and veg. The stalls are an endearing feature of the island, used for disposing of surplus garden produce – from cut flowers and new potatoes to giant marrows, courgettes and asparagus. You choose what you want and leave the correct change in an honesty box.

'Hedge veg' produce is often available at local honesty stalls.

The road from here wriggles round the western end of the airport and joins the main road. Turn right to continue west, past the Longfrie Inn (where the indoor Fun Factory is a hit with youngsters).

PLEINMONT HEADLAND/ WEST COAST

Keep heading west towards the coast and at the next junction, turn left and park in the car park on the

Sculpture in the gardens at Bruce Russell & Son's.

left-hand side of the road to explore the headland at the northern tip of **L'Erée Bay**. Just up from the car park, after the German bunker, there is a small sign on the right to **Le Creux ès Faies ⑤**, the island's third largest megalithic tomb. The name means 'Cave of the Fairies and it was believed that fairies came out on moonlit nights to dance on the nearby Catioroc headland. The tomb is surrounded by a granite wall of alternate vertical and horizontal stones, and you can crawl into the dark interior to look up at the two massive stones capping the whole structure. The prehistoric passage grave was probably built around 3000BC and continued in use for 1,000 years or more, with bodies and ashes being placed in the chambers, along with gifts of pottery, flint and stone tools.

High on the headland beyond the dolmen is **Fort Saumarez ⑥**, which has the appearance of a World War II artillery control tower. The wartime structure was constructed on top of an older Martello Tower, built in 1805. The fort is named after Lord James Saumarez, who in 1794 defeated five attacking French frigates with his ship, HMS *Crescent*. The headland

Le Creux ès Faies: a dolmen you can crawl inside.

commands fine views of sweeping Rocquaine Bay to the south and Les Grandes Rocques to the north.

LIHOU ISLAND

Continue downhill from the tower and you will come to another car park with a large monument commemorating those who lost their lives when *MV Prosperity* foundered on the reefs off Perelle Bay in January 1974 with the loss of all 16 crew. From the car park, a path leads down to the causeway which at low tide links mainland Guernsey to **Lihou Island ❼**. This lovely windswept islet, the most westerly point of the Channel Islands, is now a nature reserve noted for its seabirds and wildflowers. For centuries the causeway was one of the main gathering places of *vraic* (pronounced 'rack') or seaweed, for use as a fertiliser on farmlands bordering the coast. Horses and carts were formerly used for transport, gaining ac-

cess to beaches via the slipways. Today you can still see tractors loading up with the weed.

A notice at the head of the causeway gives the times when it may safely be crossed (the tide returns swiftly, and can cut you off). You can also find the times of the tides in the *Guernsey Press*, at Fort Grey or at www.gov. gg/lihouisland. Heights of the tide may vary, and it is advisable to err on the side of caution. The island is often exposed and can be chilly even in summer.

Once on the island, take the path to the left of the house, which now offers group accommodation. Along the path you'll come to the remains of the 12th-century priory of **Notre Dame de Lihou**, built by Benedictine monks who arrived from the Abbey of Mont St Michel in around 1114. Three dolmens and seven menhirs discovered by the monks were used as foundations for the chapel. The priory is believed to have been used until the 16th century, after which it became a farmhouse. During World War II the church was used as target practice by the Germans. Little now remains of the building, except a

The German Occupation tower Fort Saumarez.

The view from Guernsey across to Lihou Island, with its one and only house.

few wall fragments. Until 1994, when the States of Guernsey bought the island from the owners for £435,000, a Guernsey law forbade all but islanders to make the crossing to Lihou. Beyond the priory, on the northwest coast, you can climb over rocks to the **Venus Pool**, large and deep enough to bathe in, but take heed of the signs discouraging access during the nesting season. Keep to the shoreline if you want to see the best of the wildlife. But be sure to get back across the causeway before the tide cuts the island off once again!

Little remains of Notre Dame de Lihou priory.

RAMSAR SITE

Lihou Island, La Claire Mare Nature Reserve and the Colin Best Nature Reserve – 1,045 acres (426 hectares) in all – were designated a Ramsar site in 2006. Ramsar is the name of an Iranian town on the southern shores of the Caspian Sea where, in 1971, 34 countries signed the Convention on Wetlands of International Importance, aimed at promoting the conservation of threatened wetlands and their resources. Guernsey's site encompasses a variety of habitats, from shingle banks to marshes, reed beds, saline lagoons and the inter-

way alone. The saltmarsh attracts shelduck, little ringed plover, greenshank and occasional rare migrants such as the pectoral and buff-breasted sandpiper.

The Colin Best and adjoining Claire Mare nature reserves are located east of the Fort Saumarez Headland. Yellow horned poppies grow on the landward side of the shingle bank, called **Les Anguillières**, and sea kale grows on the seaward side. The fields on the opposite side of the road served as Guernsey's first airport and alongside there is an area of wet meadows and ponds, a habitat for snipe, kingfishers, wagtails and warblers.

PERELLE BAY

Continuing round the headland, stop in the next car park at the southern end of **Perelle Bay**. Perelle derives from the Celtic word for rock; at low tide the bay is a rocky lunar landscape. This used to be a favourite bay for collecting ormers, the indigenous mollusc prized for its

tidal area with its outlying reefs and rocks. The rich biodiversity of flora and fauna includes a wide range of sea birds, wild flowers and marine organisms; 214 species of seaweed have been recorded on Lihou cause-

The Guernsey cow

Guernsey cows, with their doe eyes and dished (concave) faces, are a special breed that has been selected since the mid-19th century. Hardy, and yielding large quantities of creamy fat-rich milk, the cattle on Guernsey were widely exported in the 1920s and 1930s, and are the genetic source of herds found in Australia, New Zealand and the Americas. The purity of the breed has been guaranteed by the ban on the import of live cattle to the island. The Guernsey Dairy produces cheese, butter, ice cream and the renowned thick and golden Guernsey cream.

The milk from a Guernsey cow has a high level of beta-carotine, which gives it that lovely yellow colour.

The common spotted orchid flowers in July and August.

unique flavour and mother-of-pearl inner shell. Once a staple of island dinner tables, the ormer is now a gourmet rarity, although the stocks are protected to ensure the molluscs' survival.

Cross the road to find the dolmen called **Le Trépied**. This prehistoric passage grave was reputed to be the place where local witches met with the devil for Friday-night revelries. According to confessions extracted from the "witches" at the trials in the early 17th century, the devil, in the form of a black goat, would stand on the dolmen while the witches danced round.

ST APOLLINE'S CHAPEL

At the next junction, turn right (inland) and follow the road around the sharp left-hand bend. Soon afterwards, stop to admire the lovely little **St Apolline's Chapel** ❽ (open daylight hours; free). The granite chapel, built in 1394, is a single-cell building and thought to be the only remaining medieval chantry chapel in Guernsey. The fragments of frescoes are thought to depict the Last Supper and Christ washing the Disciples' feet. The chapel had been used as a cowshed before the States of Guernsey bought it in 1873 and rescued it from this humble role. The site was restored in the 1970s as a Chapel of Unity. It is the only chapel in the British Isles dedicated to Apolline, a deaconess martyred in AD 249, who is regarded as the patron saint of dentistry.

ST SAVIOUR

Continuing inland, take the second main turning right to follow a wind-

Le Trépied dolmen dates from the Neolithic period (4000 to 2500BC).

A stained-glass window depicting St Apolline.

ing road up past **St Saviour Reservoir ❾** to the hilltop parish church. Hikers will appreciate the pleasant 2-mile (3km) walk around the reservoir. The impressive Parish Church of St Saviour is medieval in origin, and was partly rebuilt in 1658 after the spire was struck by lightning.

Turning left will bring you to the entrance of **St Saviour's Tunnels** (closed to the public for safety reasons), a complex built during the World War II Occupation that burrows beneath St Saviour's church. The Germans chose this site for their main ammunition store, reasoning that the RAF would be unlikely to bomb a church, or even suspect what lay beneath the churchyard.

Eating out

Auberge du Val
Sous L'Église, St Saviours, tel: 01481-263 862; www.aubergeduval guernsey.com; closed Sun dinner and all day Mon.
Very popular traditional *auberge* in an attractive rural setting. Ideal for a simple bistro-style lunch or more adventurous evening meals. ££

The Farmhouse
St Saviours; tel: 01481-264 181; www.thefarmhouse.gg; lunch and dinner.
In a hotel converted from an old farmhouse, the restaurant has a contemporary look and modern cuisine to match. A meal might start with a soup or seafood platter, followed by lobster and prawn linguini or free-range pork loin. Light lunches can be enjoyed by the outdoor pool in summer. ££–£££

Mint Brasserie and Tea Room
Le Gron, St Saviours (in the gardens of the Bruce Russell & Son

Goldsmiths complex); tel: 01481-266 556; www.mint.gg; Mon–Sun 9am–5pm; Fri and Sat 9am–5pm, 6.30–10.30pm.
This farmhouse-style brasserie has won favour with its fair prices, home-made cakes and scones, and à la carte lunches and dinners. The restaurant promotes locally sourced ingredients where possible, and makes its own bread, Guernsey *gâche* (fruit loaf) and traditional Guernsey bean jar (see page 12) – along with imaginative fish, meat and vegetarian dishes. £–££

Taste of India
Sunset Cottage, L'Erée; tel: 01481-264 516; www.tasteofindiaci.com; lunch and dinner daily.
Stroll across the beach then stoke up at this Indian restaurant, just across from the bay, and enjoy the sunset. Expect large portions, tasty dishes and plenty of punters. Takeaways are available. Also has a branch at 2 Mill Street, St Peter Port. £

Wildflowers frame the view across Vazon Bay.

Tour 5

Northern Guernsey

Explore the north for its fine bays, harbours and coastal forts. If you're visiting the attractions and taking breaks at beaches allow a day for this 21-mile (34km) tour.

Flat northern Guernsey has an entirely different character from the southern and central uplands. Fringed by sandy beaches, the west-facing coast is backed by dunes and sandy common, too poor to farm, but now used as a public golf course. There are plenty of opportunities for bathing so bring swimming costumes and towels. Inland, the region is more heavily developed, with industrial complexes around St Sampson's and greenhouses producing cut flowers.

TALBOT VALLEY

Head out of St Peter Port along Grange Road and The Queen's Road, past the whitewashed stucco of Regency terraces, followed by the pink granite farmhouses as you go west

Highlights

- Vazon Bay
- Fort Hommet
- Cobo Bay
- Saumarez Park
- Folk and Costume Museum
- Le Déhus Dolmen

past the Princess Elizabeth Hospital. Turn right at the next major junction to drive down the green **Talbot Valley ❶**. Part of the way down this steep-sided valley, grazed by sandy-brown Guernsey cows, you will pass Guernsey's only working watermill on the left. This is one of six mills in the valley, surviving in various states of repair.

Further down on the right is a car park in an abandoned quarry and a footpath, the **Ron Short Walk** (named after a past chairman of the Guernsey National Trust), which climbs the valley edge and affords good views over an undeveloped, peaceful and green part of Guernsey.

VAZON BAY

At the bottom of the valley, **King's Mills** is named after three watermills

that once stood on this site, drawing on the power of the Talbot Valley stream. Turn left when you reach the main road, then take the next main right turn to descend to sandy **Vazon Bay** ❷, deservedly one of Guernsey's most popular beaches. Beneath the vast sands lie the remains of a submerged forest, evidence of which is exposed periodically by winter storms. The forest is thought to have been destroyed by a tidal wave

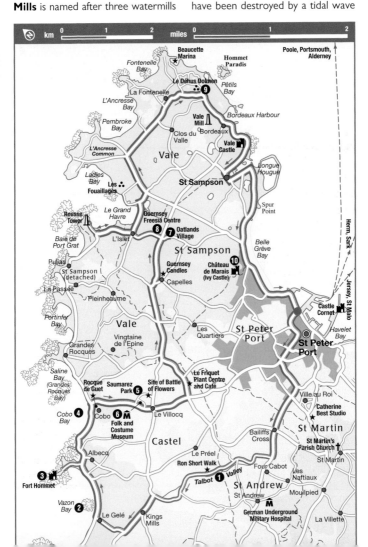

in AD709. Vazon is the sports playground of the island, where Guernsey beach boys ride the rollers and shore fishermen bring in bass and mullet. To join the fun head for the Guernsey Surf School (tel: 07911 710 789; www.guernseysurfschool.co.uk) which offers coaching for all abilities and hires out wetsuits, surf- and bodyboards, kayaks and stand-up paddleboards. As well as being a good windsurfing bay, the wide flat beach is used for motorbike racing in summer.

Fort Hommet ❸, a solidly built Martello tower of red granite, stands on the headland. to the north of the bay. Wherever you find Napoleonic fortifications, there are sure to be German defences, for the Occupation troops appreciated the skills of their predecessors in finding sites from where artillery could cover a large sweep of coast. Here, a German gun casemate (Apr–Oct Tue and Sat 2–5pm; charge) has been restored.

COBO BAY

Continuing round the coast, you next come to **Cobo Bay** ❹, another fine

Cobo Bay's distinctive pink granite is evident along the beach.

bathing beach, particularly popular with families. As evening falls, BBQs light up along the beach and diners gather on the terrace of the **Cobo Bay Hotel** to watch the setting sun. The distinctive pinky-red rock along the coast here is known as Cobo granite and has long been a source of

Fort Hommet was stripped of all scrap metal after the war.

Rara wraps

Guernsey wraps, the all-in-one beach towelling tubes, have been a tradition for islanders of all ages for over 50 years. Tying at the neck, they provide an easy and discreet way of undressing on the sands when you go for a dip at one of Guernsey's many bays. Originally all home-made, the wraps are now produced commercially – sometimes with cartoons, dragons, dolphins or other designs. The main manufacturers of the wraps are Rara at La Lisière, Bordeaux, Vale, www.rarawraps.com.

stone for buildings on the west side of the island; St Matthew's Church at the southern end of the bay is quite a striking example of its use. If you climb the steps to the top of the now-wooded quarry behind the bay, you will find the **Rocque de Guet Watchhouse and Battery**, a Napoleonic watchtower, from where there are splendid views of Vazon, Cobo and Grandes Rocques bays.

SAUMAREZ PARK

From Cobo Bay turn inland along the main road. In just over a mile (1.5km), turn left at the crossroads, and left again for the main car park of **Saumarez Park** ❺ (daylight hours; free; not to be confused with Sausmarez Manor in St Martin). Children are in their element here, with a big adventure playground, excellent tea-rooms and a vast park.

Saumarez Park and the imposing French-style house at its southern edge were created in the 18th century by William Le Marchant before coming, through marriage, into the hands of the de Saumarez family. The entire property was purchased in 1938 by

the States of Guernsey, and opened to the public.

The house is nowadays the Hostel of St John, used as a residential home for the elderly, with no access for the public. Formal gardens surround the house, very much in the same French idiom as the house itself. Both reflect the tastes of St James Vincent de Saumarez, the fourth lord Saumarez, who spent much of his life as a diplomat in the British Embassy in Paris. As well as formal gardens, there is a camellia lawn, bamboo walk, and Japanese walk and garden that James de Saumarez created on his return from diplomatic visits to Japan. He came back with many exotic plants – plus a Japanese carpenter and gardeners to build the Japanese temple and tend the grounds.

FOLK AND COSTUME MUSEUM

To the rear of the house, beyond the tearoom, is the National Trust of Guernsey's recently upgraded and

Although Saumarez House is closed to the public, you can enjoy a stroll around the gardens and the park.

The boat reputed to have saved 13 passengers from a shipwreck.

extended **Folk and Costume Museum** ❻ (www.nationaltrust-gsy.org. gg; mid-Mar–Oct daily 10am–5pm, last entry 4.15pm; charge). This excellent museum, within 18th-century farm buildings grouped around a cobbled courtyard, shows life on the island as it used to be around 100 years ago. The first part contains a series of

A mangle at the Folk and Costume Museum.

reconstructed rooms showing a typical Guernsey farmhouse kitchen, and the town house parlour of a middle-class home with period costumes and furnishings. Upstairs a display on childhood includes a school room, complete with school benches.

Every year sees different exhibitions from the wonderful costume collection, with selections from the 8,000 pieces. It could be 18th-century wedding gowns, dresses worn by film stars, island uniforms or underwear worn during the Victorian and Edwardian eras.

The outbuildings display a wide range of tools and implements used in domestic and working life in Guernsey at the turn of the century. There are crab pots, fish baskets, ormering hooks, a Victorian mangle used by children doing the washing, rabbit traps and pig-killing knives, milk cans and threshing tools, old-fashioned boneshakers and carts and carriages, all giving an insight into the varied diet and the never-ending pattern of work involved in rural life. There are even some renovated pig sties.

Fisherman's smock at the Folk and Costume Museum.

The last display is devoted to the once-flourishing tomato industry. Guernsey's first glasshouses, built in 1792, were used for growing dessert grapes but became a source of huge wealth as tomatoes, introduced in 1865, took over. Until the 1960s the sweet, juicy and flavoursome Guernsey toms (along with Jersey Royal potatoes) were eagerly awaited by many people as early-season crops. In 1957 more than 9 million 12lb (5kg) trays of tomatoes were exported. But what was once a staple of English grocers was driven out of the market by Dutch imports, and today Guernsey toms are virtually unavailable off the island.

The boat in the courtyard outside was reputed to have saved 13 passengers from the SS *Stella* which hit the rocks off Alderney in March 1899, with the loss of 105 passengers and crew.

RETAIL THERAPY

Turn left out of the museum and at the second crossroads left turn for **Le Friquet Plant Centre and Café** (www.lefriquetgardencentre.gg; Mon–

Thur 8.30am–6pm, Fri–Sat 8.30am–8pm, Sun 10am–5pm), a huge and colourful garden centre, with children's indoor and outdoor play areas, a Pets and Aquatics centre and a good café.

This is just one of a cluster of attractions in the vicinity that are ideal for rainy days. Turning right from Le Friquet, and right at the next junction, you will pass three further attractions. **Guernsey Candles** (tel: 01481-249 686; daily 9am–5pm) has candles in every conceivable shape and size as well as displays on the intricacies of the candlemaking craft.

At the next junction, the right turn will take you to **Oatlands Village** ❼ (www.oatlands.gg, daily 9.30am–

Becoming a local

If you fall in love with Guernsey, and fancy living here, you need to be rich. A glance at estate agents' windows will reveal that there are two types of property on the market, the local market and the open market. One two-bedroom apartment may be priced at £435,000, whilst its identical neighbour costs well over £1 million. The cheaper apartment can only be bought by a Guernsey native, whilst the millionaires' property is for sale on the open market. By this means, Guernsey controls migration to the islands, which would otherwise be flooded by tax exiles.

A charming cottage with tile roof will require deep pockets.

Fun at the Folk Museum

To keep children occupied at the Folk and Costume Museum there are two sets of work sheets, one for the under 10s, and another for 10–13 year olds. Youngsters fill in the forms as they go round the museum, spotting the relevant items and collecting facts and figures. Those who correctly fill in the sheets receive small prizes. Work sheets are usually handed out at the entrance; if not, ask on arrival.

Handmade dolls on display at the Folk and Costume Museum.

5pm) with attractions for all ages. Gift shops and craft workshops are grouped around a courtyard set in converted brickworks, complete with bottle-shaped kilns. Diverse attractions over the 5-acre (2-hectare) site include an attractively landscaped mini-golf course, a Jungle House play area (charge) with a soft play zone and eight full-size trampolines, Junior Go-Karts, Guernsey Goldsmiths, a large

The Oatlands kiln is a reminder of the once-thriving brick industry.

craft and hobbies shop, a *chocolatier* and a variety of eateries.

At the same crossroads, the left turn takes you to the **Guernsey Freesia Centre ❽** (daily 10am–5pm, closed Sun off season), where you can see freesias at different stages of bloom. You can also arrange to have flowers sent to friends and family at home. Guernsey produces two thirds of all freesias sold to mainland Britain, along with huge numbers of roses. Apparently the high light levels enjoyed by the island encourage the growth of long straight stems – perfect for cut flowers. Depending on the time of your visit you can see the various growing stages of the freesia, the planting of corms and the picking, bunching and boxing of the flowers.

GRAND HAVRE AND L'ANCRESSE COMMON

Due north of the Freesia Centre is the sheltered and sandy beach at **Le Grand Havre**, separated by an area of seaweed-covered rocks from the equally attractive **Ladies' Bay**. White sands here are only fully revealed in their glory when tides are low. While here, you can visit the **Rousse Tower**, which stands on the headland to the west of Le Grand Havre. One of

The Guernsey Freesia Centre is mainland Britain's key supplier.

a chain of 15 towers built in the 1780s against the threat of invasion by France, it has been fully restored and contains displays on the history of Napoleonic-era fortifications on Guernsey.

From the high points on **L'Ancresse Common**, at the very northern end of the island, you can see many such fortifications. Here the horizon bristles with tall circular towers and square forts, spaced at regular intervals, each one guarding a possible landing site and intended as a show of strength to deter

Napoleon from planning an invasion. Far harder to see is the oldest prehistoric site on Guernsey, hidden among the gorse and bracken on the southern edge of the common (ask a golfer for directions to the fifth green, but don't get too excited). Named **Les Fouaillages**, this roofless burial chamber, consisting of a ring of fallen stones, was constructed more than 6,000 years ago and only rediscovered in 1976.

At the north of the island, the adjoining **Pembroke** and **L'Ancresse Bays** form one huge stretch of flawless beach. With white sands, watersports and clear blue waters this is arguably the island's best bay, but it is often windy and at low tide you might run out of steam pursuing the sea hundreds of yards down the slope of sand. There are beach cafés at either end where you can sit and soak up this lovely stretch of coastline, and if it's too cool for swimming or sitting alfresco there are footpaths in either direction for a bracing walk. The bays provide the last opportunities for bathing, as the island's northern road fringes the common

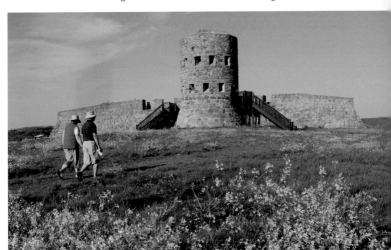

The Rousse tower and battery are a uniquely combined structure.

Vale Castle

Between Bordeaux and St Sampson's harbours, just inland from the main road, lie the hilltop relics of Vale Castle. The earliest occupant of the hill is believed to have been a double-banked hill-fort dating from the Iron Age. The first medieval fort was erected in around 1400. Barracks were constructed during the Napoleonic Wars but demolished by the Germans during the Occupation. It's worth walking up to the top for the fine views of all the Channel Islands.

Vale Castle was used as a military site for more than 2,000 years.

and turns south. From here on, the beaches are subject to fast currents – more appealing for rock pooling and birdwatching.

LE DÉHUS DOLMEN

The northeastern corner of the island is defended by the 19th century **Fort Doyle**, truncated and modernised by the Germans. More modernity can be found in the sleek yachts at Beaucette Marina, an all-weather harbour blasted out of the island's bedrock.

The passage grave at Le Déhus Dolmen is lit for visitors.

Just after the road turns south, look for a narrow lane on the left, which leads to **Le Déhus Dolmen ❾** (open 24 hours), Guernsey's most atmospheric passage grave. Not only is the dolmen perfectly preserved, with a small wooden door for an entrance, it is also furnished with an electric light. Turning on this light throws into relief a mysterious carving on the underside of one of the tomb's massive capstones: the figure of a bearded man, armed with bow and arrows, known as the Guardian of Le Déhus. Some scholars have suggested that the figure was already carved on the stone before it was incorporated into the tomb. If so, it would predate the construction of the dolmen, which is itself more than 4,000 years old.

Continuing south, you will see the tall tower of **Vale Mill** (1850) high on a hillock over to the right as you skirt the fishing port at Bordeaux Harbour. Originally a flour windmill, the occupying Germans used it as an anti-aircraft position.

ST SAMPSON

The former industrial hub of the island has been spruced up in recent years and has a well-equipped marina. But it is still a commercial working harbour with shipyards, a power station and oil tankers, and given that St Peter Port is just down the road there is not a lot to detain the tourist. The best known retail outlet for visitors is **Ray & Scott**, who specialise in diamonds and have their own diamond museum (Mon–Sat 9.30am–5pm).

As a last stop, before returning to St Peter Port, look out for the Château de Marais standing on the edge of a drab housing estate inland from Belle Grève Bay. Known locally as the **Ivy Castle** ❿ (open daylight hours) it is no longer ruined and ivy-clad, but has been well restored to illustrate a sequence of defences, from the 13th-century moated bailey to the 18th-century powder magazine and the inevitable concrete bunker, built when the Germans re-fortified the castle during World War II.

Eating out

The Beach House
Pembroke Bay, Vale; tel: 01481-246 494; www.beachhouseguernsey.com; open all day in season.
A café and restaurant right on the beach in a stark modern building, with a viewing gallery for meals above. Open for breakfast through to dinner. £–££

Cobo Bay Restaurant
Cobo Bay Hotel, Cobo Bay; tel: 01481-257 102; www.cobobayhotel.com; lunch and dinner except Jan and Feb when closed for lunch.
The panoramic windows of this seaside hotel make the most of the beach views and sunsets. Start with diver-caught scallops wrapped in pancetta and follow with chargrilled beef fillet or home-made veal burger. The restaurant has won awards for the quality of food and service. ££–£££

Cobo Fish and Chip Bar
Cobo Bay; tel: 01481-254 276.
Buy fish and chips from this basic but popular chippie and enjoy them while watching the glorious sunset over Cobo Bay across the road. £

Crabby Jacks
Vazon Bay, Castel; tel: 01481-257 489; www.crabbyjacksrestaurant.com; daily noon–9pm, Fri and Sat until 9.30pm.
A casual seaside bar and bistro popular with surfers and families for its large helpings of steaks and burgers, king prawns and poached mussels, and at night for its fabulous sunset view. £

Fleur du Jardin
Kings Mill, Castel, tel: 01481-257 996; www.fleurdujardin.com; lunch and dinner.
This country hotel produces first-class, simply cooked gastro pub fare, with an emphasis on local produce. Expect Guernsey-bred beef and pork, freshly caught seabass, west coast scallops or a locally sourced crab sandwich. Regarded by many as the best dining pub in the Channel Islands. £–££

Surfside at Port Soif
Port Soif, Vale, tel: 01481-253 709; daily 9am–4pm.
Excellent value home-made food including bacon butties, fresh crab sandwiches and generously buttered Guernsey gâche. £

Roc Salt Beach Café and Restaurant
Mont Cuet Road, Chouet, Vale, tel: 01481-246 129; www.rocsalt.gg; closed Mon and Sun dinner.
A recent addition to the north of the island's culinary scene, Roc Salt has become a popular choice for fish and steak and has a balcony with fine views over Chouet Bay.

The Rosaire Steps.

Tour 6

Herm

This diminutive island with enticing beaches and no cars makes a wonderful day or half-day trip from Guernsey. The 3-mile (5km) walk covers most of the island.

Herm is a tiny holiday island measuring just 1.5 miles (2.5km) long and 0.5-mile (1km) wide. Visitors come for the scenery, the swimming, the walking and the wildlife. It's also a favourite of foodies who come over from Guernsey for lunch or on the early evening boat to enjoy freshly caught lobster or Sark lamb.

Freedom from consumer values is what makes Herm so appealing and, with a ban on cars, radios played in public and unseemly behaviour, this really is the place to get away. The best way to enjoy all this peace is to walk around the island.

Beach lovers begin to arrive in mid-morning in summer, heading for the broad swathes of sandy beach to the north and east. Although the is-

Highlights

- Fisherman's Beach
- Shell Beach
- Belvoir Bay
- St Tugual's chapel

land has enough paths and beaches to absorb most of the tourists, try and avoid Sundays in high season when the boats are packed with day-trippers from Guernsey.

The only way of getting to Herm is by boat. Travel Trident passenger ferries (tel: 01481-721 379, www.travel trident.com) depart from St Peter Port harbour and take 20 minutes. Tickets can be bought at the Trident kiosk by Weighbridge Clock Tower (near the

Liberation Monument) or from the boat crew as you board. In July and August ferries depart eight times daily from 8.30am–5.15pm. Boats run all year but there is a reduced service off-season (six boats in spring and autumn, limited trips in winter) and services are dependent on the weather. Last boats back are at around 5pm but there are special seasonal 'dinner boats' returning at 10.45pm if you want to go for an evening meal. For all other information on Herm, visit www.herm.com.

HERM HARBOUR

At high tide ferries dock in Herm's small harbour, while at low tide passengers disembark at the Rosaire Steps before making their way along the track to the harbour – which is the hub of the island. The long-established **White House Hotel ❶**, overlooking gardens and beach, is a country house hotel with an old-fashioned charm and sense of decorum. A stay here is an escape from the 21st century – there are no televisions or telephones in the bedrooms and no clocks on the walls.

From the harbour, a broad level path leads left, passing the **Mermaid Tavern ❷**. This was originally a fishermen's pub; now it is the social centre of the island. The path was once a railway that carried stone from the island's numerous quarries to cargo boats in the harbour. Herm's granite was said to be the hardest and best of all stone quarried in the Channel Islands in the 19th century. It was used for railway construction as well as for more prestigious projects: in London, the Duke of York steps, leading off Pall Mall, and the steps up to St Paul's Cathedral are both made of Herm granite.

To the left, as you follow the path, is **Fisherman's Beach ❸**, a fine

Fisherman's Beach.

stretch of sand at low tide, when you can also see the weed-covered crates in which Herm's oysters are grown. The first main landmark on the northwards route is a small cemetery containing two graves and an almost indecipherable inscription; local legend has it that this is the grave of a mother and child who died of cholera in the early 19th century, buried here by the crew of a passing ship.

HERM COMMON

Much older tombs lie scattered around **Herm Common ❹**, at the north end of the island, but it is not easy to distinguish them from natural scatters of rock, since these Neolithic tombs, dating from the period 3,500 to 2,000BC, have all collapsed – only the regularity of the stones, lying in a rough circle, indicates the site of a former tomb chamber.

There were once so many tombs here that archaeologists think Herm was used as a burial isle for members of Breton nobility. Most were lost over time to 19th-century quarrymen; the big granite capstones of the Neolithic passage graves were easy picking.

The common has more than 450 species of wild flowers. It is covered in burnet rose, a rare plant that enjoys the Herm environment, as well as all kinds of other wild flowers, from massed primroses in spring, to fuschia-pink foxglove spires in summer, and more exotic plants like New Zealand flax and Japanese cactus.

The needle-shaped monument at the northernmost point of the island

The Pierre aux Rats obelisk sits on the northern shore of Herm.

marks the position of one of the island's more famous dolmens, called the **Pierre aux Rats**. When quarrymen destroyed the massive grave, the local seamen were incensed at the loss of such an important landmark and navigational aid, so the obelisk was erected in its place.

Gearing up for the beach

If you come to Herm unprepared for the beach, head for the shop near the harbour where you can buy swimming costumes, snorkels, skimboards, fishing gear and other beach paraphernalia, all at reasonable cost. Don't forget suncream – Herm has the highest incidence of sunburn in the Channel Islands. The post office here sells Herm stamps, which have become collectors' items. The Guernsey PO took over Herm's postal services in 1969 and Guernsey stamps are nowadays used for post from the island.

Local stores can provide everything you need for a day on the beach.

SHELL BEACH AND BELVOIR BAY

Over to the right lies **Shell Beach** ❺, backed by dunes where prickly sea hollies grow. With almost 0.75 mile (1km) of golden sands and superb swimming, this is considered by some to be the Channel Islands' best beach. It consists almost entirely of shells, though most have been pulverised to fragments of sand by centuries of wave action. Each tide brings in a new crop of delicate pink, yellow and luminescent shells to keep beachcombers happy. As you explore, however, you will discover that Shell Beach is by no means unique: all the island's beaches have a large amount of shells, as does the island soil – Herm is just one big trap for exotic shells washed here from warmer waters by strong currents and the action of the Gulf Stream.

The clear and shallow waters retreat far out at low tide, making swimming safe for children. Beach cafés both here and at Belvoir Bay sell snacks, deliciously creamy ice creams and all the essential beach paraphernalia.

The calm waters and white sands of Shell Beach.

If you continue round the coast, you will come to **Belvoir Bay** ❻. This has a smaller but more sheltered beach than those further north, and has lovely views of Sark and (on a clear day) France. It is perfect for swimming but the sands can get very crowded in summer. From here you can head south along the undulating (and at times steep) cliff path, which

A footpath leads through wild flowers down to Belvoir Bay.

On foot is the only way to get around the island.

encircles the island and gives access to some of the best birdwatching points.

WILDLIFE

Even if you are not a bird lover before you go to Herm you may well become one once you reach the island – it is a good idea to take binoculars and a bird identification book. The island is especially rich in birdlife during the spring and autumn migration periods, when the Channel Islands serve as a feeding ground for birds of passage. During spring and summer, the whole island is alive with the vibrant song of larks, wrens and warblers. The cliffs to the south of the island attract nesting puffins and fulmars, while the sand dunes to the north are home to a colony of sand martins and, if you arrive by the early morning boat before the beaches become crowded, you will see whole flocks of oyster catchers, probing the sands for food with their bright orange beaks. In spring and early summer, the local branch of the RSPB (www.rspbguernsey.co.uk) organises puffin patrols and trips to Herm or you can take a two-hour

puffin-watching kayak tour (www.outdoorguernsey.co.uk) starting at Shell Beach. The distinctive, large-beaked residents have been spotted on every patrol since 2007.

Also keep an eye out for the grey seals and bottlenose and common dolphins that have made their home in the northern rocky outcrop called The Humps.

MANOR VILLAGE

An alternative to going south along the cliff path is to head up the steep

Puffins breed on Jethou and Herm from April to mid-July.

fought with Wellington at Waterloo. He fell in love with the place in 1890 and bought the island lease. The prince introduced many trees to the island along with a colony of wallabies, which bred successfully but have since vanished. Sadly, the prince was interned at the outbreak of World War I and never returned to Herm.

A subsequent tenant was the novelist, Sir Compton Mackenzie, best remembered for *Whisky Galore* (1928) who lived here from 1920 until he retired to the neighbouring island of Jethou. He was succeeded by Lord Perry, the chairman of Ford who once lived in The White House Hotel and gave it its unique name 'in homage to his transatlantic connections'. Lampposts and cottage fronts were once painted bright blue or orange – the colours of the Ford Motor Company.

ST TUGUAL

A cluster of farm buildings and cottages lies at the top of the hill, among them the tiny junior school. A teacher commutes from Guernsey daily, in all

track to the huddle of granite houses at the centre of the island on the brow of the hill. The tower at the summit serves as a landmark as you climb. The tower and manor are the work of Prince Blücher von Wahlstatt, a wealthy and eccentric German aristocrat, the son of the Prussian Field Marshal Gebhard Blücher who

Idyllic island

Herm has a resident population of just 66. There are no nurses or doctors, although there are set procedures and selected people to deal with emergencies. Motorised vehicles are banned, with the exception of three tractors, one Land Rover and a handful of quad bikes for the locals. You can't own a house on Herm, play a radio in public areas or pick the flowers. Troublemakers used to be interned in the tiny beehive-shaped prison in the grounds of the White House Hotel. Today they are shipped back to Guernsey and the prison is used to store lawnmowers.

Unlike the other Channel Islands, bicycles are banned on Herm.

Post-war Herm

During the war, the island escaped fortification, and was largely left to decay, so that the first post-war tenant spent a small fortune restoring the island farms. Even so, much remained to be done when Peter and Jenny Wood became tenants in 1949. The story of how they fell in love with Herm and worked to create the thriving island economy of today, based on the twin pillars of tourism and farming, is told in the late Jenny Wood's delightful book, *Herm, Our Island Home*, available from the gift shop at Herm Harbour.

grain. The chapel was designed so that the monks could sit in the nave, out of sight of the congregation. When Prince Blücher von Wahlstatt arrived on the island, he found the structure in a state of disrepair. He restored the building and reopened it as a chapel.

St Tugual remains an enigma. Rumour has it that the saint was a Welsh woman who accompanied St Magloire to Guernsey and Herm in the 6th century, who died here and whose memory was perpetuated by the building of the shrine. The Wood family restored the chapel and it is used for a service at 10am most Sundays. If you would like to play the organ, speak to the manager of the White House Hotel.

LE MANOIR

weathers, to teach the handful of pupils. Nearby you can visit the enchanting little Norman chapel of **St Tugual** ❼ whose pretty garden has a memorial to Peter and Jenny Wood, former tenants of the island (see box). The chapel is a reminder of the days when Herm was a religious outpost, run by Catholic monks who founded a monastery and improved the land so it could fatten livestock and produce

Turn right out of the chapel, retracing your steps past the dismembered tractors. Turn right, up the hill. At the gate to **Le Manoir** ❽ (The Manor House) is a reminder that oxen were once used as draft animals before Lord Perry introduced the first tractors. The **oxen stocks** were used to hold the animals while they were shod, since, unlike horses, bullocks are unable to stand on three legs, and need supporting.

St Tugual church dates from the 10th century.

Climbing the Rosaire Steps after disembarking from the ferry.

may have been built by the medieval monks who farmed the land on Herm until the 16th-century Dissolution. The monks also built the walls of massive granite boulders that line the spine road crossing the centre of the island.

Follow the road and you will pass the island's campsite on your left and eventually rejoin the coastal path at the southern tip of the island. Turn right here, enjoying the views across to Jethou, and you will come to **Rosaire Steps** ❾ used by Herm ferries as an alternative landing point when the receding tide makes it impossible to use the main harbour. The path now skirts the gardens of the White House Hotel, backed by the cliffs formed by quarrying activity in the 19th century. Drunken quarrymen were incarcerated in the small **gaol** by the tennis courts on the grounds of the hotel, which merits inclusion in the *Guinness Book of Records* as Britain's smallest gaol.

Alongside the manor you will see another tower, made romantic with fairy-tale turrets, that was once the island's mill. Like the chapel, it

Eating out

Conservatory Restaurant
White House Hotel, Herm Harbour; tel: 01481-750 075; usually daily for lunch and dinner; closed Nov–Mar.
Traditional hotel restaurant with fine views across to Guernsey and glorious sunsets. Meals on the lawn in fine weather. Extensive wine list, with many brought directly from Bordeaux châteaux. ££–£££

Mermaid Tavern
Herm Harbour, tel: 01481-710 170; Apr–Oct daily, restricted times off-season and closed Nov–Mar.
The social hub of the island, with pub lunches and a good choice of beers and wines. This is the venue of the occasional real ale and cider festivals. At the Black Rock Grill (evenings only)

steak and fish are cooked on volcanic rocks at your table. The meat choice ranges from beef fillet to ostrich and wild boar. £–££

The Ship Inn Brasserie
White House Hotel, Herm Harbour, tel: 01481-750 075; open in season daily from 9am.
Serving excellent cuisine from the kitchens of The White House Hotel, the Ship Inn has a more informal atmosphere than the Conservatory Restaurant. Come for a fry-up breakfast, seafood or sandwich lunch, cake and cream teas, cocktails or full dinners with good-value wines. Meals can be taken alfresco on the patio, in the bar by the log fire or in the restaurant. £–££

Fishing

For Channel Islanders, fishing has always been a way of life. Lobster, crab and scallops, along with bass, brill and bream, are still all caught offshore and end up gracing the table.

The limpet shells discovered at La Houge Bie, a Neolithic passage grave in Jersey, are evidence that even back in prehistoric times the islanders were enjoying their seafood.

During the Middle Ages eel was a favourite dish; the drying, salting and export of conger eels was the main industry of the Channel Islands and led to Jersey's nickname of 'Isle of the Congers'. In the 16th century canny islanders recognised the riches of the cod banks of Newfoundland, and made fortunes by sailing to Spain with huge quantities of dried cod, returning to the islands with fruit and wine. The home fisheries consequently declined but the industry was revived in the late 18th century when oysters were discovered and exported in huge quantities to England.

THE SHELLFISH FLEETS

Fishermen gradually turned their focus to lobster and crabs. String upon string of baited lobster pots were lowered to the kelp-covered reefs by fishermen from sturdy crabbers; then bigger boats ventured further afield, seeking their valuable quarry in the English Channel and even off the Scottish coast.

Creels are used to bring in the catch on a number of local fishing boats.

Fishing on the net

www.fishing-guernsey.co.uk
Useful site regarding species you can catch and where and when to fish for them. Also covers charter boat hire, tackle and bait shops and angler-friendly accommodation.
www.boatfishing.net (tel: 07781-104 356). Out The Blue angling trips with skipper Richard Seager, holder of the Guernsey boat brill record. He takes you to the best spots for bass, turbot, pollack, brill, bass and bream.
    See also under Angling in Active Pursuits, page 110.

The 1960s saw the shellfish boom, with lobsters and crabs fetching high prices in top-end restaurants. Crabbers still bring in the shellfish, but meanwhile other forms of commercial fishing, such as trawling, have declined. This has, however, been good news for the sea angler.

SEA ANGLING

Sea angling is now a major leisure activity. The Bailiwick of Guernsey has about one fifth of all British shore records; Alderney has an international reputation as a shore fishing centre where record-breaking ballan wrasse and monster grey mullet are landed. April to September are the best months for serious boat fishing. Depending on the tides you could be bank fishing for turbot, bass and brill, wrecking for cod, conger and ling or reef fishing for pollack, bream or bass. Late summer or early autumn are ideal for shore fishing for bream, bass, sole, red mullet, triggerfish, plaice, wrasse, conger and garfish, while autumn to early winter is best for wrasse and mullet.

LOW-WATER FISHING

Rock pools are a haven for crabs, crayfish, shrimp and devil fish. At strictly enforced times of the year you can seek out the ormer, which are valued by locals for their meat and by tourists for their fine mother-of-pearl interior shells. At very low tide you can sprinkle salt on the key-holed burrows of razor fish, wait for them to pop up (they will think the tide is in), then pull them from their holes.

Long-lining a horse through Sark's lanes.

Tour 7

Sark

Step back in time and spend a day on this idyllic island. Motorised traffic (apart from tractors) is banned, so hire a bike for this 10-mile (16km) tour, or trust to your own feet.

Victor Hugo considered Sark to be *'la plus belle'* of the Channel Islands. See if you agree by taking a day trip to the island, or go for an overnight stay. Ferries to the island are run by the Isle of Sark Shipping Company and depart from St Peter Port on Guernsey, taking 50 minutes. Spring and early autumn are good times to visit, although Sark is very popular with families in the summer months. Queue early if you want outside seating on the ferry. In high season there are several boats a day, but it's wise to book ahead, especially if you decide to day trip on the cheaper 'early bird' sailing, departing at 8am and returning at 4pm or 6pm (book online at www.sarkshippingcompany.com). If you decide to stay on the island there are

Highlights

- St Peter's Church
- La Seigneurie Gardens
- La Coupée
- Silver mines
- Venus Pool

comfortable hotels ,B&Bs or self-catering cottages. If you're looking for a more basic option, there are a couple of attractive campsites.

Sark is a small peaceful island with the atmosphere of Victorian England, and that's what attracts visitors. It has a population of 600 and the head of its government (or Chief Pleas) is the seigneur. Sark's constitution dates back to 1563, when Helier de Car-

The Isle of Sark.

teret was granted sovereignty over the island in return for maintaining a militia, whose chief task was to keep the island free of the pirates who had been using Sark as a base from which to harass English shipping. Helier took 40 Jerseymen with him to colonise the uninhabited island. He divided Sark into 40 parcels of land and granted perpetual tenancy to the occupants in return for their help in defending the island. These tenements, as they are known, have remained virtually unchanged. The feudal form of government set up in Elizabeth I's reign prevailed right up until 2008 when the island held its first general election and Sark became Europe's newest democracy.

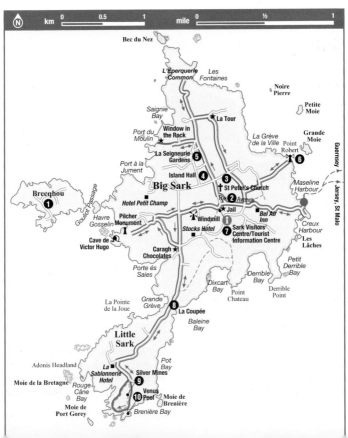

BRECQHOU ISLET

The ferry passes south of Herm before swinging northwards past the rocky islet of **Brecqhou** ❶. This was sold by Dame Sybil Hathaway, the most famous ruler of Sark, in 1929 for £3,000 and purchased in 1993 for a reputed £2 million as a private tax haven by the reclusive billionaire Barclay brothers, best known as owners of the Telegraph media group and The Ritz. To the shock and horror of the Sarkese, the tycoon twins created a massive mock-Gothic castle on the island, complete with 100ft (30-metre)

Sark Shipping Company ferry arriving at Maseline Harbour.

On your bike

Sark is only 3 miles long and 1.5 miles wide (5km by 2.5km), so on a bike you can explore it all in a day. Bikes can be hired cheaply from Avenue Cycle Hire on The Avenue. In season it's best to book in advance (Avenue Cycle Hire, tel: 01481-832 102; www.avenuecyclessark.co.uk or A to B Cycles, tel: 01481-832 844; www.atobcycles.com). Apart from the occasional steep hill, pedalling is easy going. To explore some of the bays and rocky shores you have to leave the bike (no need to lock up) and continue on foot. If you're scrambling around the coastline do be aware of the state of the tide.

Cyclists taking in the view from Sark across to Brecqhou.

-high granite walls, battlements and helipad. The castle is clearly visible as the ferry swings to the north of Sark. There is no public access.

Having bought the property, the brothers were forced to pay the seigneur of Sark his *Treizième* or one-thirteenth of the purchase price of a tenement, under Sark's jurisdiction over Brecqhou. The brothers were also dismayed to learn that, under Sark law, they were obliged to leave the estate to an eldest son. Demanding the right to bequeath the property to all four of their children, they threatened to take the battle to the European Court of Human Rights. In 1999 the Chief Pleas caved in and updated the constitution.

In 2008, against the wishes of the majority of the islanders, the Barclay brothers instigated the first full election on Sark. Up until then the Chief Pleas (Sark's government) had mainly comprised members who had inherited their seats under the island's 450-year-old feudal system of government. When the majority of voters rejected the Barclay brothers' preferred candidates and their manager in Sark lost his seat in the new Chief

Climbing a coastal pathway gives an excellent view across to Brecqhou.

Pleas office, they withdrew their £5-million annual investment in Sark. Their family businesses on the island, including hotels, pubs and shops, were temporarily shut down and Sark workers laid off.

The bitter feud continues, particularly between the Sarkese and the owner and editor of the controversial *Sark Newspaper* with scathing attacks on the island's local politicians and on Sarkese whom he believes are sympathetic to the administration. The Barclay Brothers own around a quarter of Sark and continue to seek the full defeudalisation of the island. The paper has compared the government to fascist Germany in the 1930s and refers to the seigneur as the 'unelected feudal lord'. The editor, previously head of the Barclay Brothers owned Sark Estate management, closed down four of their hotels on the island in 2014 and 2015, and all still remain shuttered.

ARRIVAL IN SARK

The ferry comes in close beneath Sark's towering cliffs, past rocks where cormorants and shags launch themselves on fishing flights. As you approach the harbour, you may see fishermen laying crab and lobster pots, and numerous sea caves and evocatively shaped rocks.

From the sea there are few signs of human habitation, for Sark's houses lie mainly at the centre of the island, in a sheltered hollow, hidden from sight as you approach by sea. Settlers here in the 16th century built their homes as far inland as they could to shelter from the elements and from unwelcome visitors. To this day, most of the Sarkese live without a sea view.

If you're staying on the island, luggage will be carried off the boat by a team of porters who will take it

The 'toast rack' will carry you from the harbour up the steep hill.

Horse and carriage, the only other approved form of transport.

to your accommodation. Make sure your bags are labelled clearly with your name and accommodation.

To reach the main village, you can either hop on the 'toast rack' – an open-sided tractor-drawn cart, which makes light of the short but steep haul up Harbour Hill – or take the pretty woodland footpath which runs alongside the road. At the top of the hill, footpath and road merge at the Bel Air pub.

HORSE-DRAWN CARRIAGES

At La Collinette, just beyond the toast-rack stop, the island's famous horse-drawn carriages patiently wait to take visitors on tours around Sark (£10 or £15 per person for one or two hours respectively, ask for discounts for children. In high season you can pre-book an island tour when booking the ferry crossing.) Formerly the only powered vehicles permitted on the island were the invalid car belonging to Dame Sybil Hathaway and the tractor attached to an ambulance-van for medical emergencies.

There are now more than 70 tractors, which are used for agricultural purposes and cargo deliveries. The doctor visits his patients by tractor and the ambulance is still the back end of a conventional ambulance towed by a tractor. For visitors, horse-drawn carriages are the only kind of transport allowed, apart from bikes. For the more energetic, cycling is the best way to see Sark, especially as not all the horse-drawn carriages can cross the narrow isthmus of La Coupée to Little Sark. Since this is not a round-the-island tour (there is no main coastal footpath) the suggested tour of 10 miles (16km) can easily be cut for those who prefer a shorter route.

BIG SARK

Sark's main road, **The Avenue** ❷, is lined by souvenir shops, bike hire outlets and café/bistros that are open all day for snacks and casual meals. If you are planning a picnic, you can find provisions at one of the food stores here. (Note that although there are two banks, Sark has no ATMs. Most of the shops and restaurants, however, take

St Peter's is the last church in Britain to rent pews, although the price has not increased since 1820.

wooded lanes lead to La Coupée, the vertiginous land bridge linking what are often described as the separate islands of Little and Big Sark.

At the top of the Avenue, note the post box opposite the Post Office, painted gold in 2012 to celebrate local resident Carl Hester's gold medal win for his part in the British Olympic Dressage team. Turn right to join the main track going north. You will shortly come to **St Peter's Church** ❸, built in 1820. The simple building has stained-glass windows of various saints, including St Magloire, who came from Dol in Brittany in 565 to found a monastery on Sark. The monastery flourished, supporting 62 monks and serving as a school for the children of the Breton nobility, until marauding Viking pirates destroyed the buildings and killed the monks in the 9th century.

Turn right out of the church, and after the Old Island Hall on the same side of the road you'll pass a stone building which houses the **Assembly Room** where the Chief Pleas' meetings take

credit and debit cards, and some operate a cashback system for up to £50).

The Avenue divides the island into two halves – to the north are the La Seigneurie Gardens, to the south,

Island wildlife

Sark's isolated position brings a wealth of wildlife. Among the bird species you are likely to see along the rugged coast are puffins, shags, guillemots, razorbills and oyster catchers. For the best sightings bring your binoculars and take a trip around the island with local fisherman, George Guille. You will sail past spectacular rock formations, visit caves with deep, clear water and secret beaches and coves that can only be reached by sea. Boat trips are best taken on a calm day when the caves are accessible. Trips depart from Creux Harbour at 11am and must be pre-booked (tel: 01481-832 107).

A local advertisement for a group bird-watching tour around the island.

place four times a year. Sark's feudal state came to an end in 2008 when the Chief Pleas was reformed and Sark held its first election (see page 83). Continuing along the road you will see the **Island Hall ❹** on the left which, with its indoor sports (badminton, pool, indoor bowling, snooker and table tennis), café and bar, serves as a centre for much of Sark's social life.

LA SEIGNEURIE GARDENS

A little further north, you will be sharing the road with horses and carriages heading to and from **La Seigneurie Gardens ❺** (www.laseigneurie gardens.com; Easter–Oct daily 10am–5pm; charge, guided tours every Wed at 11.30am), home of the new Seigneur of Sark, Christopher Beaumont (great-grandson of Dame Sybil Hathaway) who took over the role when his father, Michael Beaumont, died in 2016. Seigneurs of Sark have traditionally allowed public access to the gardens of the 17th-century home. Although Sark is no longer a feudal state and the powers of the seigneur are much eroded, he still holds the is-

Gates decorate the entrance to the gardens at La Seigneurie.

land in perpetuity for the Crown, sits in the court of Chief Pleas and pays the Queen an annual rent of £1.79.

The sheltered **walled gardens** are packed with colourful flowers and shrubs, including climbing roses and exotic plants such as gazanias, canna lilies and bottle-brush plants from New Zealand that flourish in the frost-

The high walls around La Seigneurie Gardens protect delicate flowers.

Point Robert Lighthouse stands guard on the cliffs of Sark.

free island environment. The house it-self (not open to the public) is no less exotic, with the Dutch gables of its Victorian wing added to the original house of 1732 and a large watchtow-er built, so it is said, for sending signals to Guernsey in 1854.

Displays in the recently renovat-ed chapel tell the history of Sark's Seigneurs and the Seigneurie. To the rear of the great house is the Battery, where a cider apple crusher and sever-al historic cannons are displayed along-side an ornate tower, and a turreted 18th-century dovecote. Until relative-ly recently one of the seigneur's sole privileges was to keep pigeons and doves, which fed freely and with impu-nity on the crops of the tenants.

PORT DU MOULIN AND THE LIGHTHOUSE

A short way along the track north of La Seigneurie is a left turn that leads down, through woods, to **Port du Moulin** (once the site of a water-mill), with its fine coastal scenery. Just before you get to the beach, look out for the artificial 'Window in the Rock', a square hole perhaps cut through the

cliff to allow carts to descend to the beach and gather *vraic*, or seaweed, used for fertilising the seigneur's fields and garden. Returning to the main track, you can turn left and contin-ue to the end of the road to **L'Ep-erquerie Common**, at the north-ern tip of the island, named after the poles *(perques)* once erected here for drying fish.

Dark Sky Island

Tiny Sark was designated as the world's first Dark Sky Island in 2011 by the Dark-Sky Association, in recognition of the exceptional blackness of the night sky. The isolated location, lack of public street lighting and a ban on cars account for the truly dark skies. The Sark Astronomy Society (SastroS; www.sastros.sark.gg) was formed by a group of enthusiasts eager to share their stargazing experience. An observatory has opened for stargazing activities; those interested in using the telescopes with a guide should enquire at Sark's Visitor Centre (tel: 01481-832345).

Saving the seagulls

One of Sark's many ancient laws forbids the shooting of seagulls, because of the guidance the birds' cries gave mariners when the wind dropped and their nesting rocks and headlands vanished into sudden sea mists. Until the mid-19th century, when it was finally conceded that another war with France was unlikely, the way into Sark's harbours was a closely guarded secret.

Seagulls tend to live communally, in large, noisy colonies.

Coming back, turn left down Rue de Fort, to the Napoleonic-era defensive works at **La Tour**, then head south, back towards the centre of the island. Take the second left turn, which leads

past the Mermaid Tavern down to Point Robert and Sark's **lighthouse** ❻ (closed to the public). It was built in 1912 and stands halfway down the cliff into which it nestles, via a flight of 165 steps, but still 213ft (65 metres) above high water mark. It is now automatic; the platform offers superb views of Maseline Harbour and on a clear day, you can see all the way to France.

THE PRISON

Return to The Avenue, turn right, passing the shops and then left at the end of the main street. You will see, beside the **tourist information centre** ❼, a curious stone building with the prominent date of 1856: this is the two-cell **island prison**, built to hold miscreants at a time when Sark's quarrying industry – and the incidence of drunkenness and violence – were at a peak. Today the Sarkese locals take it in turn to become the Connétable (special constable) who oversees the gaol. The Connétable and his assistant, the Vingtenier, have the power to retain offenders in the gaol for two nights, after which they have to be released or transferred to Guernsey. Continue along the road for about a third of a mile (0.5km) and turn left, heading south for Little Sark.

The window-less jail can house two prisoners.

La Coupée is slowly being eroded; eventually Little Sark will be an island.

A left turn at the next junction leads down to Stocks hotels, and beyond it, Dixcart Bay. This is a worthwhile detour if you have time, but bear in mind that you can't get to the bay by bike. A beautiful woodland path leads to the valley bottom. You can follow the stream here on foot until it reaches the bay, a fine sandy spot for bathing when the tide is out.

LA COUPÉE

Continuing south the path bears right and the razor-edged isthmus known as **La Coupée** ❽ comes into sight. Linking the two parts of the island and looking just like a miniature stretch of the Great Wall of China, this is Sark's most famous landmark. A roadway tops this knife-edge ridge, some 10ft (3 metres) wide – too narrow for a horse and carriage but you can easily take a bike across; a notice warns cyclists to dismount while crossing. To either side there is an almost sheer drop of 260ft (80 metres) straight to the sea. Crossing La Coupée was once extremely hazardous and schoolchildren had to crawl across the causeway in high winds, but as the plaque in the middle

of the causeway relates, the path was made good with concrete and handrails in 1945 by German prisoners of war. The steep flight of steps leading down from the north end of La Coupée to the lovely **Grand Grève** beach on the right was closed after a landslide in 2010. The cost of repair is prohibitively

Grand Grève beach is no longer accessible.

Caragh Chocolates

If you're looking for a gift from Sark, stop at Caragh Chocolates, on the left after La Coupée, coming back from Little Sark. These mouthwatering chocolates are handmade and many of them (such as 'Sark cream and double chocolate ganache' or 'Sark cream and tiramisù') contain the rich, pure (and famous) local cream. Tea gardens on the premises are open daily 10am–5pm for light lunches and cream teas with home-made cakes. There is also a pool (for a small charge) so don't forget to bring your swimming costume.

Caragh chocolates make a great gift for those back home.

expensive, but on an island with so few sandy beaches, this is a great loss.

LITTLE SARK

Enjoy the views of the neighbouring islands as you follow the sunken lane to **La Sablonnerie**, a fine hotel with a restaurant and charming tea gardens, and the ivy-covered ruins of an old mill nearby. Turn left by the hotel and continue along the track until the tall granite chimneys and ruins of Sark's **silver mines** ❾, growing out of the wild bracken and brambles, come into view.

Silver was discovered on Sark in the 1830s and Cornish miners were brought over to work it. The mines produced both silver and copper, but not in sufficient quantities to be an economic success. Ten miners were drowned in 1845, and two years later, when the galleries collapsed and flooded, the ill-fated mining company went bankrupt.

Go through the gate, leave your bike and head towards the first of the chimneys, then follow the path as it bends left. Take care as these paths take you close to the cliff edge. The objective is to reach **Venus Pool** ❿, a large natural rock pool at the base of the nearby cliffs. The 10ft (3-metre) -deep pool is uncovered for 2.5 hours either side of a low tide and visitors frequently fail to find it (ask locally about the tides and check the way). When the grass runs out and gives way to bare granite, cairns mark the best route. Reaching the pool involves a scramble, but you can pay homage to the goddess of love by bathing in the pool, or you can enjoy the many other smaller tide pools with their crystal-clear waters. The gold-tinted flat rocks around it are suitable for sunbathing.

To return to La Coupée simply retrace your steps. Back on Big Sark, carry straight on along the main track, until you reach a crossroads after about half a mile (1km).

The remains of an abandoned silver mine from the 1830s.

The first left leads to the **Pilcher Monument**, built to commemorate Joseph Pilcher, who drowned while crossing to Guernsey in a storm in 1868. There are fine views back to Guernsey. The right turn opposite leads down Rue de Moulin, named after the **windmill**, built in 1571. In use until 1919, it stands at the highest point on the island, at 365ft (111 metres), and just a step away from the island's main street.

If you have time when returning to the harbour, turn right and go through the rock-cut tunnel, dug in 1588, to view Sark's original dock, pretty Creux Harbour, which was replaced by the modern port, La Maseline, in 1947.

The window in the rock was made to give a view of Les Autelets rocks.

Eating out

Hathaways
La Seigneurie Gardens; tel: 01481-832 209; www.laseigneuriegardens.com; daily 10am–10pm
The combination of the setting in the grounds of La Seigneurie and the top-notch cuisine makes this one of Sark's most appealing places to eat out. The menu is modern and eclectic with European influences and a hint of the Orient but using local fresh produce wherever possible. Some dishes on the menu even include the name of the fisherman or farmer who supplied the ingredients. Three-course dinners, with generous helpings, all home-cooked and well presented, are good value. It is open all day for cream teas, at lunch time for light meals and in the evenings offers a full restaurant menu. ££

La Sabonnerie
Tel: 01481-832 061; www.la sablonnerie.com; lunch and dinner, closed in winter.
Located in the south on peaceful Little Sark, this is the perfect place to stop on a walking or cycling tour. You can enjoy snacks, cream teas and seafood platters in the flower-filled tea gardens or a gourmet lunch in the restaurant, based on the ingredients produced on the hotel's organic farm. For guests at this charming old farmhouse, or others staying in Sark, there are candlelit dinners. Roasted sea scallops, lobster Thermidor or fillet of home-grown beef can be followed by crème brûlée with a montage of exotic fruits and berries. £££

Stocks
Tel: 01481-832 061; www.stocks hotel.com; lunch and dinner.
This charming country house hotel is renowned for its cuisine. Choose from à la carte, table d'hôte or lobster menus and make the most of the fruits of Sark's seas: mackerel, pollock, seabass, Sark crab and hand-dived scallops. Lobsters are caught daily within a three-mile radius of the hotel. For carnivores there are home-smoked meats, foie gras, steak and Sunday roasts. Leave room for delicious desserts and end the day with Sark sloe gin or apple brandy. £££

A shopping street in St Anne.

Tour 8

Alderney

Unwind on this peaceful little island caught in a time warp. The 13-mile (21km) tour, either by bike or car and foot, takes a whole day.

Alderney lies just 8 miles (13km) west of Normandy, and the cobbled streets of its only town, St Anne, have a distinctly Gallic atmosphere. Some 3.5 miles (5.5km) long and 1.5 miles (2.5km) wide, it has cliffs to the south but to the north it slopes gently down to a series of beautiful sandy bays.

The island has largely escaped mainstream tourism and remains quiet and unspoilt, with a friendly and relaxed atmosphere and a refreshing lack of bureaucracy. It certainly feels very different from Jersey or Guernsey – it is much more sparsely populated and quite remote. There are more than 50 miles (80km) of footpaths and walks around the island, and it's a haven for bird-lovers and ornithologists.

Highlights

• St Anne
• Alderney Society Museum
• Braye
• Alderney Railway
• Mannez Lighthouse
• Burhou Island
• Les Etacs

Islanders from Guernsey and Jersey come for beaches, golf, quirky shops and – last but not least – the restaurants and watering holes. The islanders have a reputation for conviviality and there is a definite emphasis on taking time out to eat, drink and be merry. If you're tired of walking Alderney's wind-blasted cliffs in a squall, sitting in a warm pub is the best thing to do. The pubs are more like clubs – full of character and characters, and the natural place to be on an island that offers few places of entertainment. Alderney stole a march on Guernsey by being the first to allow publicans to open on Sundays.

Alderney's character differs somewhat from the other islands, partly because it was deliberately depopulated during World War II and used as a forced labour camp. The island was massively fortified by the Germans; relics of the Occupation can be seen along the coastline.

Alderney is small enough to feel like an island, with the sea nearly always in view, yet large enough for day-trippers to leave feeling that they could have done with a little more time. If you decide to stay overnight there are several hotels and guesthouses.

This day tour of the island can be covered either entirely by bike, or by a combination of car and foot. If time is limited there are regular bus tours of the island, available on certain days, or taxis that offer affordable tours.

A German watchtower.

GETTING TO ALDERNEY

The fastest though not the cheapest way to visit Alderney from Guernsey is to hop across by plane. Flights are operated by Aurigny (see page 115) and take just 20 minutes. Alderney Airport was the first officially recognised airport of the Channel Islands, opened in 1935, and still not much more than a few prefab huts and a hangar. Going by sea (www.bumble

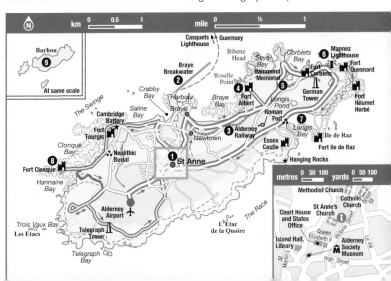

Capital shopping

The shops in St Anne are delightfully quirky. No high street stores or Starbucks here, but family butchers and bakers, shops selling fishing tackle, bric-a-brac and sweets in old-fashioned large glass jars. As in France, all the shops close down for a two hour lunch break. If you're feeling the breeze, walk down to Channel Jumpers in Braye Street where you can buy traditional Guernsey and Alderney sweaters.

An old-fashioned greengrocer's shop in St Anne.

bee.gg) is a cheaper option, but the boat takes 1 hr 25 minutes and only departs from Guernsey on Fridays and Sundays (from May to October).

For the energetic visitor, hiring a bike is a good way of seeing the island (Cycle & Surf, St Anne, tel: 01481-822 286, www.cycleandsurf.co.uk, or Auto-Motion, Braye Harbour, tel: 01481-823 352, www.automotion derney.com). You can't cover the entire island in a day on foot, but there are some wonderful walks and distances between the main landmarks

A plaque in Victoria Street commemorates the monarch's visit.

are easily walkable. Taxis will be waiting at the airport for round-the-island tours (ABC Taxis, tel: 01381-823 760, Island Taxis, tel: 01481-823 823). You can also hire a car (Braye Hire Cars, tel: 01481-823 881; www.brayehire cars.com). Driving couldn't be easier: no traffic lights, no road rage and not much traffic.

ST ANNE

The capital, **St Anne ❶** (referred to by locals simply as 'town') is an attractive maze of cobbled streets lined by houses of granite and sandstone, many of them whitewashed or painted in lovely pastel shades. **Victoria Street**, named after the monarch who visited Alderney on 9 August 1854, has most of Alderney's shops and restaurants. It's worth popping into the **Alderney Visitor and Wildlife Information Centre** for some excellent walking guides.

Just south of the information centre is the entrance to **St Anne's Church**. This massive French-style building of local granite, with Caen stone details, was designed by Sir George Gilbert Scott in 'chaste Gothic' style, and opened in 1850. It replaced the old church, which was described at the time as 'small

St Anne's Church.

ALDERNEY SOCIETY MUSEUM

The tower and churchyard stand near the **Alderney Society Museum** (Easter–Oct Mon–Fri 10am–noon and 2.30–4.30pm, Sat–Sun 10am–noon; www.alderneysociety.org; charge), which is housed in the former Old School, founded in 1790 by the island's governor, Jean Le Mesurier. The museum provides a detailed account of the island, from its geology and wildlife to such topics as whether the Alderney cow ever existed as a distinct breed.

One section deals with wartime Occupation and the evacuation of all but a handful of the island's population. From 1942–4 Alderney was used as a forced labour camp with almost 5,000 labourers from all over Europe transported here to turn the island into an impregnable fortress. The labourers toiled in harsh conditions; several hundred of them died from starvation and brutality. Alder-

and mean'. The body of the **Old Church** was demolished, but you will find the squat tower, which survived, and the old churchyard, containing some fine 18th-century tombstones, by continuing to the top of Victoria Street and then turning right into the High Street.

Cannon found in an Elizabethan wreck, Alderney Society Museum.

ney had the only concentration camp on British soil during the war, with 1,000 inmates from Sachsenhausen concentration camp transported here to work on fortifications.

When the Alderney residents were allowed to return in the winter of 1945, they had to agree to work cooperatively, under central management, to restore houses and farmland left derelict by the occupying forces. Hard work and self-sacrifice saw the island economy restored within two years, but there were moments of farce, as illustrated by the infamous Battle of the Butes. This took place in 1945 after British troops, preparing for the islanders' return, cleaned out their homes and stacked such furniture as had survived in the open air, with a rope barrier. A free-for-all broke loose once the rope was removed, with islanders fighting each other for their possessions. For decades after, it is said, some people on the island refused to invite others into their homes for fear that their guest might recognise a family heirloom.

Another section of the museum displays artefacts salvaged from the Elizabethan warship, the 60ft (18-metre) *Makeshift*, wrecked off the coast of

Alderney and discovered in 1977 by a fisherman. Apart from a cannon, pottery and leather clothing, two of the most intriguing finds are early tobacco pipes – one made of pottery and one of pewter – with tiny bowls, reflecting the fact that tobacco, introduced to Europe only two decades previously, was still a very expensive luxury.

ISLAND HALL

Close to the museum are some of Alderney's oldest buildings: turning right just beyond the museum will take you into Connaught Square, with the Old Government House of 1763, now better known as **Island Hall** where States of Alderney, the island parliament, used to hold its meetings. It is now the seat of the States' civil service department. The imposing Georgian building was originally constructed as a private house for the Le Mesuriers, the hereditary governors of Alderney, who clawed their way to wealth and status through acts of licensed piracy. In one year alone during the wars with France, Jean Le Mesurier, under a licence granted by the English Crown, captured shipping valued at £135,000 – a fortune in the late 18th century.

Island Hall, where Alderney parliament used to hold its meetings.

Braye Harbour has one of the longest harbour walls in Europe.

BRAYE

From the centre of St Anne it's just a few minutes' walk down the hill to Braye Harbour. The great sandy sweep of Braye beach is protected by the Alderney breakwater and therefore offers sheltered bathing. The harbour is safe from the strong current of the Swinge, just off-shore. For all its small size, Braye has more than its fair share of places to eat, from chip shops and pubs to upmarket seafood restaurants.

THE BRAYE BREAKWATER

Along with Alderney's ring of 12 defensive fortifications, the **Braye Breakwater ❷** is a legacy of the suspicion that existed between England and France in the early 19th century, even though hostilities officially ceased after the defeat of Napoleon. When the French began constructing a naval harbour at Cherbourg, alarm bells rang in the Admiralty, and the British government suddenly decided it was urgent to build 'harbours of ref-

The Alderney spike girls

Only on Alderney are you ever likely to see a blonde hedgehog. These creamy-coloured, flea-free creatures, with beady button-black eyes, have a rare recessive gene. There is a population of around 1,000 on the island and they have been breeding here since a couple of them were released in the 1960s – allegedly from a Harrods shopping bag. You are most likely to see them at dusk or in the early morning.

The blonde hedgehog is not an albino, it has a recessive gene.

Cricketing ties

Alderney has strong links with well-known cricketing characters. John Arlott, once His Master's Voice of BBC cricket commentaries, retired to Alderney in 1981 saying it was a 'desperately easy place' to live in with a 'pleasant absence of bores'. Ian Botham was a regular player here and had a holiday home on the island. Since the 19th century cricket has been played on Les Butes, a spectacular pitch with sea views.

Visiting teams tend to stay for Saturday only, playing a shortened version of the game.

uge' at Braye on Alderney, as well as on Guernsey and Jersey. The intention was to convert Braye harbour into a massive naval base, with a breakwater at each side of the bay. Only the western wall was built, completed in 1847 and originally a mile (0.5km) long. Battered by massive waves (signs warn walkers that the wall is liable to sudden swamping by breaking waves), part of the breakwater was abandoned and now lies submerged beneath the waves, a hazard to shipping.

Today local fishermen cast their lines from the breakwater, and during winter storms locals congregate here to watch the waves crash dramatically against the wall.

THE ALDERNEY RAILWAY

The **Alderney Railway** ❸, one of the oldest in the British Isles, was constructed in the 1840s by the British government to convey stone from Mannez Quarry to build the breakwater and the forts. The first official passengers were Queen Victoria and Prince Albert, who were carried in 1854 in a horse-drawn tender.

At weekends and on bank holidays from Easter to September, the railway carries passengers on a 2-mile (3km) trip from the harbour up to the northeast coast, a journey of 15 minutes (departures at 2.30pm and 3.30pm on Sun in May–June, Sat and Sun in July, Sun in September; for information tel: 01481-822 978 or visit www.alderneyrailway.com). Passengers are either carried in a diesel-powered railcar, or in one of two 1938 London Underground carriages. The bright red tube carriages shuttling beneath the gorse- and bracken-covered hills of Longis Common make a bizarre sight.

THE NORTHEAST COAST

A circular road hugs the northeastern coast, forming a loop from Braye back

An abandoned rail line along the Braye harbour breakwater.

Fort Albert affords wonderful views of the marine life in Braye harbour.

to St Anne. Following the Lower Road east out of Braye, you will skirt Braye Bay and encounter **Fort Albert** ❹, the first in the chain of 12 fortresses encircling the island, designed in the 1840s and 1850s. Suspicious of French intentions, the English imported hundreds of English and Irish labourers to construct these fine fortifications of pink granite, but most were never subsequently garrisoned. Several have now been converted into private flats and holiday apartments, while others remain in a decayed and dangerous state – best appreciated from afar. Fort Albert is perhaps the finest of them all, and is well positioned to defend Braye Harbour.

HAMMOND MEMORIAL

A short way on, the road divides; the spot is marked by the **Hammond Memorial** ❺ commemorating the many prisoners of war who died on Alderney during the Occupation period. They were imported to work as slave labourers on the construction of the defences that were to turn the Channel Islands into the most heavily fortified area in Europe. Plaques in Hebrew, Polish, Russian and Spanish indicate the origins of those who lost their lives: Spanish partisans who were on the losing side in the Civil War, Jews from Alsace and Czechoslovakia, and prisoners of war from Russia and Poland.

SAYE AND CORBLETS BAYS

Fork left at the memorial for **Saye Bay** (pronounced 'Soy'), an idyllic horseshoe-shaped white-sand beach between rocky headlands. Children

Corblets Bay offers excellent swimming and surfing.

The Mannez Lighthouse beam is visible 23 miles (37km) out to sea.

love leaping off the rocks here – and in summer it's popular with campers from the island's only campsite just over the dunes. The next beach along is the delightful **Corblets Bay**, with clean sands and shallow waters. This is the best beach on the island for surfing and bodyboarding.

MANNEZ QUARRY AND LIGHTHOUSE

Evidence of quarrying activity lies all around the northeastern tip of the island at **Mannez Quarry**, close to the railway station terminus. Above the quarry stands the large and sinister fire control tower, built by the Germans to act as a command post for the various artillery batteries around the island. It is known locally as The Odeon. From here there are clear views across to the Cap de la Hague in Normandy. Mannez Pond at the eastern end of the quarry provides a rich habitat for wetland birds as well as Alderney's nine species of dragonflies. **Mannez Lighthouse** ❻ (tours every Sunday pm from Easter to Sept; charge) is Alderney's most

conspicuous landmark. It was built in 1912 to aid vessels along this treacherous stretch of coast.

LONGIS BAY

Continuing round the coast, another fine stretch of sandy beach is found at **Longis Bay** ❼. Additional shelter is provided by the massive concrete anti-tank wall. This was partially constructed by the Germans, who were convinced that the Allies would eventually try to retake the Channel Islands by landing tanks and troops. The structure remains incomplete. At the far end of Longis Bay, an attractive château-like building, known locally as **The Nunnery**, stands on the site of Alderney's Roman fort. It was here that the coins, pottery and bronze work in Alderney Museum were excavated, while much of the museum's Iron-Age material came from a site on the adjacent golf course. Just to the north, **Longis Pond** has a bird-hide, information point and bird feeding area, perfect for ornithologists.

HANGING ROCKS

The Nunnery marks the point at which Alderney's lowlands give out. Just to the south, the cliffs rise steeply

Longis Bay features an uncompleted tank wall and sandy beaches.

Puffin webcam

The Alderney Wildlife Trust's puffin webcam (www.teachingthrough nature.co.uk) streams live footage of puffins on the island of Burhou. The best time to check out the puffins is during the afternoon and early evening. From June onwards you may see adults returning with fish and sand eels for their growing chicks. The site also features a puffin forum and information on the birds and their habitats.

Puffins are often called 'sea parrots' due to their colourful beaks.

to the landmark known as the **Hanging Rocks**. Here, two huge boulders look as if they have detached themselves from the cliff and are about to tumble into the sea. One local legend has it that Jerseymen, jealous of Alderney's beauty, once tried to tow the island closer to their own by attaching a rope to the rocks; all they succeeded in doing was to tilt the rocks. **Essex Castle**, now private flats, stands high above the rocks, while the main road leads straight uphill, back to St Anne.

SOUTH OF THE ISLAND

The southern part of the island can only properly be explored on foot or by bike, since the best parts of the coast are only accessible by paths. Allow a couple of hours for this 5-mile (8km) exploration of the southern cliffs and take binoculars for spectacular views of gannetries.

If you are coming from St Anne, start at the church and take the western exit from the churchyard. Turn right to follow the road called La Vallée down to the sea at Saline Bay. Turn left to follow the coast road, past **Fort Tourgis**, derelict for 30 years.

Take the road to the right of the fort to follow the coast. The surfaced road soon gives way to a track, leading to **Fort Clonque** ❽, built in 1854 and sited on an offshore islet. The fort has been converted to holiday apartments by the Landmark Trust (see page 126). You can only access the fort when the tide is out, as the causeway is covered by water at high tide. The intertidal rocks at Clonque Bay are perfect for rock pooling. At the northern end, the wreck of the SS *Emily Eveson* reveals itself at low tide.

Fort Clonque stands on its own rocky island.

Les Etacs

The islands lying offshore are called Les Etacs (also known as Garden Rocks). What looks like snow covering these rocky islets is, in fact, a colony of gannets, which first arrived on the rocks in 1939. The colony expanded rapidly during the war. Now about 7,000 pairs nest here from spring, departing again every autumn. Les Etacs and nearby Ortac rocks support more than 2 percent of the world's gannet population. From the southern coast you can also see the islands of Sark, with Brecqhou to the right, then Herm and Guernsey.

The gannet is a protected species in the United Kingdom.

You can then walk out and look inside its boiler, but beware of the tides.

BURHOU ISLAND

From Fort Clonque you can see across to the tiny uninhabited **island of Burhou** 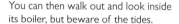. With no rats, no cats and very little human disturbance, the island is a haven for breeding sea birds, including more than 120 breeding pairs of puffins. In 2005 the island and surrounding wetlands were granted Ramsar status (see page 58) to protect the birdlife and marine species.

Burhou has a closed season from mid-March to 1 August but there are 2.5-hour boat trips on certain days in summer, to view the puffin and gannet colonies on Burhou Island, Ortac and Les Etacs and the Atlantic seal colony near Burhou Reef. You might even spot the odd basking shark in summer. For information on boat trips go to www.visitalderney.com.

SOUTH COAST CLIFFS

This is Alderney at its most beautiful and ruggedly spectacular. Follow the track known as **'The ZigZag'**, as it winds uphill, and enjoy the amazing views. Turn left at the next junction, then right onto a surfaced track, which turns back into a rough track after a short distance. Continue to the viewing point at the end of the headland, above **Trois Vaux Bay**.

There were once steps down to Telegraph Bay, but the way is now too treacherous for it to remain open.

TELEGRAPH BAY

Retrace your steps and take the next turn right. Ignore the next right, but take the right turn after that to head for Telegraph Bay. This was previously a favourite retreat for swimming and sunbathing if the tide was out, but since the steps fell into disrepair the beach has sadly been inaccessible. The bay is named after the Telegraph Tower that stands atop the headland, used in the early 19th century to send semaphore signals to the other islands.

Admire the views from the bench at the top of the bay, then return to the main track and turn right, skirting the southern side of the airport. The track bends northwards at the far side of the airfield, taking you, via La Petite Rue, back to St Anne's High Street and the centre of town.

Eating out

St Anne

Bumps Bar and Bistro
Victoria Street, St Anne; tel: 01481-823 197; closed Sun dinner off-season.
A long-standing favourite among islanders for the variety of dishes and superb fish and seafood. The chef is also the owner, which is always good news. Service is attentive and friendly, and there's a sunny patio for alfresco dining. ££

Cantina No 6
6 Braye Street, St Anne; tel: 01481-824 063; Tue–Sat 10am–10pm.
The pizzas are oustanding; otherwise try the tapas, steak or pasta, all made to order, and make sure you leave space for the cappuccino mousse. Dine inside or alfresco on the small deck. ££

Georgian House
Victoria Street, St Anne; tel: 01481-822 471; www.georgianalderney.com; lunch and dinner.
The best place to eat at this family-run restaurant is in the lovely sheltered garden at the rear of the hotel. The menu is a mix of traditional British pub and European cuisine, with emphasis on seafood, and use of local and sustainable produce where possible. Very friendly staff. ££

Jack's Brasserie
Victoria Street, tel: 01481-823 933; daily 9am–5pm.
This is a popular spot for breakfasts, light lunches and coffee and cakes. With a sunny terrace on the High Street, it's a good spot to relax and watch the world go by. £

Braye

Braye Beach Hotel Restaurant
Braye Street, tel: 01481-824 300, www.brayebeach.com; lunch and dinner.
Book a table overlooking the lovely Braye beach and tuck into turbot with pan-seared scallops, shellfish bisque or butter-poached lobster. The hotel is rated 4-star so prices are higher than average but the set menu is good value. ££–£££

Braye Chippie
Braye Harbour, tel: 01481-823 475; Wed–Sat 5.30–9pm, longer hours in high season.
Very popular, with (bookable) seating inside and out, right by the harbour. Bring your own bottle. £

First and Last
Braye Harbour, tel: 01481-823 162; closed Tue lunch.
Rita and head chef Brendan are great hosts and produce outstanding fish and seafood. Expect freshly caught lobster, scallops and crab as well as steak, poultry and home-made desserts. Quite quirky decor and harbour views. ££

Guernsey is perfect for keen cyclists.

Travel Tips

Active Pursuits

From golf and guided walks to coast-eering and kayaking, the island of Guernsey has plenty of outdoor sports and activities to keep you occupied.

With 28 miles (45km) of stunning cliff-top paths, beautiful bays for watersports and clear blue seas for fishing, there is no shortage of ways to enjoy the great outdoors. Along with long-established activities such as golf and sailing, sports enthusiasts can now try out abseiling, coasteering and other adventure activities. For full details go to www.visitguernsey.com.

WALKING

Walking opportunities are plentiful, from dramatic rugged cliffs to the leafy lanes of the interior. The most spectacular and challenging walk is the south coast footpath, which dips down to villages where you can take a break at beachside cafés. The walk can either be done in its entirety over a long day, or in separate shorter sections at a gentler pace. The scenery is best in spring when wild flowers are in bloom and birds come ashore to nest.

An extensive programme of themed walks with accredited guides runs from April to September. Guides are enthusiastic and dedicated, and provide a remarkable range of themed walks. Information is available from the Guernsey Information Centre, which also provides a series of trail leaflets and a free walking map of Guernsey.

During the Spring and Autumn Walking Weeks, guided walks focus on different aspects of Guernsey's natural beauty and heritage, with around 40 walks to choose from. The most detailed maps of the islands are the Ordnance Survey-style Bailiwick of Guernsey (1:15,000), but last updated 2010, or the Perry's official guide, which is a booklet showing every lane. When exploring the coast, watch out for extreme tidal movement, one of the largest recorded in the world. Beaches can disappear rapidly, so it's best to plan with an abundance of caution. And don't forget comfortable shoes, binoculars and sunblock.

Alderney has 50 miles (80km) of footpaths, across commons, cliffs and beaches. The Alderney Wildlife Trust organises informative guided walks throughout the year, ranging from history and heritage to birdwatching and bat walks, plus useful leaflets on self-guided walks. During Alderney Wildlife Week in May guided walks explore the wide range of habitat and species on the island, including the un-usual blonde hedgehogs. The small is-land of Sark is ideal for walking, as is its neighbouring island Herm, although there you have no other choice.

The Channel Island Way is an ex-citing 110-mile walking route incorporating the best coastal walks in Jersey, Guernsey, Alderney, Sark and Herm. With a bit of island hopping (by boat or plane) ramblers can discover one of the most beautiful and diverse

Hiking through lush vegetation.

walking destinations in the UK. Serious ramblers can do the whole route in the space of a fortnight (including the island-hops on ferries or boats). Obviously you don't have to do the whole route, nor do you have to be a super-fit walker.

Fishing for razor clams

When the tide is low children can have fun trying to catch razor fish (also known as razor clams). Go equipped with a bag of salt, walk along the shoreline and look for the keyhole-shaped burrows in the sand. Sprinkle a teaspoon of salt over the hole, wait for the clam to pop out of its burrow, then pull it gently out of the hole. The clams are slightly chewy but can be delicious if cooked correctly, ideally steamed with wine, garlic and herbs. The best beaches for collecting the clams are L'Ancresse Bay and any of the west coast beaches on a low spring tide.

Razor fish or clams have a fragile, curved shell.

One toe in the sea

If you are used to indoor pools or swimming in the Mediterranean, the Channel Island waters will feel on the cool side. In the summer months temperatures average around 63°F (17°C). This means that most beachgoers do no more than paddle, leaving the seas delightfully crowd-free for serious swimmers. The beaches are washed twice daily by the tides and the waters are clear, but beware of strong currents and rip tides.

Guernsey is blessed with clean, sandy beaches.

ANGLING

With their varied coastlines, offshore reefs and clear waters, the Channel Islands are ideal locations for sea anglers, especially from mid-summer to the end of autumn. Around 70 different species of fish are caught from the shores, including conger, rays, turbot, bass and bream. No permission is needed to fish from the coastline or harbours. A number of commercial operators offer fishing trips. Angling boat trips include *Out the Blue II* charters (www.boatfishing.net) for groups of 10–12 with a choice of wreck fishing, deep sea reef fishing, bank fishing or bass angling.

Alderney is one of the best places in the British Isles for shore fishing, with a large range of species, including turbot, mullet, ling, tope, bass, bream, plaice, sole and thick-lipped mullet. St Anne has a well-stocked tackle and bait shop which can organise lessons for the novice or young angler.

CYCLING

Fit cyclists can forget the car on Guernsey and use pedal power to enjoy the scenery. No distance is too far to cycle, though you may find the amount of traffic you encounter off-putting. The tourist board VisitGuernsey publishes an excellent free guide to waymarked cycle paths called *Guernsey Cycle Tours: 11 Island Routes*, also available online at www.visitguernsey.com/cycleguide. Routes are graded from 'Gentle & Rolling' to the more arduous 'Up Hill and Down Dale' and are designed to take in the island's tourist attractions as well as

Cyclists cross La Coupée to Little Sark.

refreshment stops. The most pleasant roads are the *Ruettes Tranquilles* (Quiet Lanes) where pedestrians, cyclists and horse-riders have priority over cars, and motorists are meant to slow down to a sedate 15mph (24kmh). Cycling is an ideal way of getting around car-free Sark (see Tour 7, page 82). For cycle hire in Guernsey, see page 117.

WATERSPORTS

Sailing and windsurfing

For sailing or windsurfing lessons contact the Guernsey Sailing Trust (tel: 01481-710 877; www.sailingtrust.org. gg). The waters are popular among yachting enthusiasts but inexperienced sailors should beware of the tides and currents. Skippered boat charter can be organised through Guernsey Boating (www.guernseyboating.com).

Surfing, scuba diving and SUPB

The rollers on Guernsey are not comparable to those on Jersey, but you can find surf on the island's west coast and on Alderney. The Guernsey Surf School at Vazon (tel: 07911 710 789; www.guernseysurfschool.co.uk) offers lessons and courses.

Conditions are good for scuba diving with clean (and cold) waters, good visibility and plentiful marine life. The Blue Dolphins Sub Aqua Club (tel: 01481-712 492; www.bdsac.org.gg), a branch of the British Sub Aqua Club, offers a range of diving experiences, including shipwrecks. Dive Sark (tel: 01481-832 565; www.sarkci.com) organises courses and dives to explore the reefs and caves around the island; book early to avoid disappointment. The clear waters around the islands are also excellent for snorkelling and swimming.

Sea kayaking is available on Cobo Bay for experienced adults.

Stand-up paddle boarding (SUPB) is rapidly growing in popularity and is enjoyed in bays around the island on calm days.

ADVENTURE SPORTS

You can abseil on the west coast as the sun sets, climb the cliffs in the morning light, or roll down the hill inside a giant transparent plastic ball (zorbing). Coasteering routes enable punters to experience the exhilaration of sea-level traversing, rock scrambling, kayaking, jumping from high rocks and swimming in gullies and caves. You just come equipped with a swimming costume, a good pair of trainers, shorts or tracksuit, and a change of clothes for later. For further information visit www.outdoorguernsey.co.uk or call 07781-130403.

GOLF

Guernsey has two 18-hole courses. The number one is the Royal Guernsey at L'Ancresse (tel: 01481-246 523; www.royalguernseygolfclub.com) in the north of the island, where visitors need to produce a handicap certificate from a recognised club. But all are welcome at La Grande Mare at Vazon Bay, Castel (tel: 01481-253 432; www.lagrandemare.com), a hotel-based course. There is also a pristine 9-hole par 3 course designed by Tony Jacklin at St Pierre Park Hotel, St Peter Port (tel: 01481-727 739; www. handpickedhotels.co.uk/stpierrepark) with tuition for all abilities.

On Alderney the 9-hole Alderney Golf Club (tel: 01481-822 835; www. alderneygolfclub.com) is a scenic and testing course, with fine views of France.

HEALTH AND LEISURE

Keep in shape at King's, a Les Mills premium club on King's Road, St Peter Port (tel: 01481-723 366; www. kings.gg), with all the latest fitness equipment, fitness classes and high-intensity training workouts. There are indoor and outdoor swimming pools, spa, sauna and steam rooms, tennis, squash and a café. Day memberships are available.

Golf course with Napoleonic towers at L'Ancresse Common.

Boat trips

Cruising around the Guernsey coast, chartering a speed boat, spotting dolphins or seals, landing mackerel or sea bass, hopping across to Herm or Sark and taking a ferry to France are among the many boating options. To see the wildlife around Guernsey, the smaller islands and offshore reefs, take a trip in a rigid inflatable boat (Rib Voyages, www.islandribvoyages.com). On Sark a boat trip is the best way to explore the rugged coast, caves and birdlife, and on Alderney to see the puffin colony and gannetries.

Visitors often enjoy a ferry trip to take in the wildlife.

The Beau Séjour Leisure Centre, Amherst, St Peter Port (tel: 01481-747 200 for sports bookings) is the place to take the family on rainy days (see page 28).

HORSE RIDING

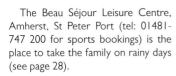

Treks and escorted hacks along bridle paths normally last two or three hours. The long-established Melrose Farm Riding School (Castel parish, Guernsey; tel: 01481-252 151) is approved by the British Horse Society (a sign of quality) and caters for all ages and standards. It has an all-weather arena overlooking the west coast and takes rides onto Vazon beach.

On Alderney you can explore scenic cliffs and country paths on horseback, and from October to March, on the beaches too. To book a ride call or text Jill Moore (tel: 07781-421 325) or email bjmoore65@yahoo.co.uk.

Late August sees the annual Alderney Horse Show, with showjumping and showing classes sharing the schedule with equine fancy dress and dog agility classes. This family-friendly show is open to all.

Horse riding on the beach is a romantic way to see the scenery.

Themed Holidays

Themed holidays on Guernsey run the range from eco-camping to gourmet weekends.

WILD FOOD FORAGING WORKSHOPS AND ECO-CAMPING

Wild Guernsey offers half-day workshops for very small groups focusing on food foraged from hedgerows, fields and seashore. Learn about sustainability, work in the wild and sample seaweed or rock samphire from the shore, pennywort (like mangetout) from the hedgerows or wild onions from the waysides. The workshops sit alongside Green Tourism Gold awarded sustainable glamping with views of the west coast, just one minute from the beach. Wild swimming, kayaking, snorkelling, surfing, guided walking and cycling can also be arranged. For details call Tara de Jersey, tel: 01481-263 153 or 07781122420 or email: wildguernsey@yahoo.co.uk.

SUMMER CAMPS

Young surfers can join non-residential summer camps with the Guernsey Surf School (tel: 07911710789; www. guernseysurfschool.co.uk). Apart from surf tuition, there is rock-jumping, beach games, kayaking, snorkelling and board design. Courses take place from July to September for 8–16 year olds.

THE WHITE HOUSE WEEKENDS, HERM

The White House Hotel (tel: 01481-750 075; www.herm.com) offers themed weekend packages from Guernsey, typically wine tasting and gourmet weekends. Packages include transport from Guernsey as well as accommodation.

WELLNESS BREAKS/ YOGA RETREATS

Rest, relax and rejuvenate with a wellness package at the Old Government House Hotel and Spa (see page 124), the St Pierre Park Hotel (see page 125) or, in Sark, Stocks Hotel (see page 126). The 4-star Fermain Valley Hotel (www.fermainvalley.com) offers occasional yoga packages, as does Power Yoga on Herm (www.poweryoga guernsey.com). For more information on yoga in Guernsey, go to www.bein-spiredby.co.uk.

Guernsey's west coast and Alderney offer some great waves for surfing.

Practical Information

GETTING THERE

Year-round air and sea packages, short breaks, flights and accommodation can all be arranged through specialist tour operators. For details see www.visit-guernsey.com/tour-operators.

By air

All visitors flying to the Channel Islands need a passport or photo ID. Regular year-round flights operate from airports throughout the UK (but not Heathrow) with added flights in high season. Flights take 45 minutes from London Gatwick and as little as 30 minutes from some regional airports. The Guernsey airline **Aurigny** (tel: 01481-822 886; www.aurigny.com) flies direct to Guernsey from London Gatwick, Stansted and City airports, Manchester, East Midlands, Leeds/Bradford, Norwich, Bristol and Southampton via Alderney; Flybe (tel: 0371-700 2000; www.flybe.com) operates flights to Guernsey from Birmingham, Southampton and Exeter. The best prices are normally secured by booking well in advance online and avoiding weekends and the busiest times of year. Aurigny provides a Channel Island hopping service between Jersey, Alderney and Guernsey; Blue Islands (now a Flybe franchise partner) links Guernsey and Jersey.

By sea

The only ferry line from the UK to Guernsey is Condor Ferries (www.condorferries.co.uk) which operates high-speed car ferry services from Poole to Guernsey all year round (3 hours). Ferries provide a cafeteria, TV room for children and duty-free shop with some excellent deals, especially on alcohol. Club-class seating is available, with reclining seats and complementary refreshments. It is not uncommon for boats to be cancelled or delayed because of the weather conditions, particularly off-season.

Aurigny is the Norman name for Alderney, as well as for the local airline.

Local buses trundle around Guernsey.

Condor also operates a slower ferry service from Portsmouth on the conventional Clipper ferry. The return crossing is overnight with the option of 1-, 2-, 3- or 4-berth cabins and en suite facilities. From Guernsey, it is a 20-minute ferry hop to Herm and 45 minutes to Sark; Jersey and Alderney are each a 15-minute flight away, or one hour by sea.

Visitors bringing their own car must have an insurance certificate, the complete vehicle registration document and a valid driving licence or International Driving Permit. Bikes can be taken across on the Condor ferries free of charge.

GETTING AROUND

Guernsey has a variety of transport options, both public and private. The smaller islands, however, leave you with little choice between a bicycle and your own two feet.

Buses

Guernsey's bus network services most parts of the island, including the main beaches and visitor attractions. Information including routes, fares and timetables can be accessed on www.buses.gg. Timetables and maps are available from the bus terminal, Visitor Information Centre or online at www.buses.gg.

Travel passes are available for 1, 2 and 7 days for individuals and families. You can hail a bus and the driver will stop to pick you up provided it is safe to do so.

Several companies operate scheduled or tailor-made bus tours, including Island Coachways (tel: 01481-720 210, www.icw.gg) and Intransit (tel: 01481-700 066; www.intransit.gg).

Le Petit Train

The new Petit Train, departing from Albert Pier, makes a 35 minute circuit around St Peter Port with a commentary on the main highlights.

Car hire

Car hire prices are similar to those in the UK, although fuel is slightly cheaper. A valid driving licence is required with no endorsements for dangerous or drunken driving in the last five years. Child seats and cars with automatic transmission cost extra. Drivers must have held a full licence for a year and must be over 20 or 21 years of age (depending on the company). There are also varying maximum age restrictions. Car hire companies in Guernsey include Avis (tel: 0808-284 0014; www.avis.co.uk) and Hertz (tel: 0800 735 1014; www.hertzci.com). On Alderney, try Braye Hire cars (tel: 01481-823 881, www.brayehirecars.com).

Driving

The rules of the road are the same as those in the UK: driving is on the left, seat belts are compulsory and it is an offence to use a mobile phone whilst driving. Fixed alcohol limits and roadside breath testing are similar to the UK.

The maximum speed limit is 35mph (55kph) and less in many areas. In towns it is 25mph (40kph) and on the *Ruettes Tranquilles* (Quiet Lanes) motorists must slow down to 15mph (24kmh). A yellow line across the junction of a minor road means stop and give way to traffic on the major road. A yellow arrow on the road warns of a junction ahead. Many junctions on Guernsey have a filter-in-turn system, marked by a cross-hatched yellow box painted on the road. You must not enter the box until your exit is clear.

Most roads are very narrow, visibility can be poor at junctions, and the lanes are used by tractors, cyclists, pedestrians and horses, as well as buses and cars, so be aware of your surroundings.

Parking often requires a 'parking clock' which can be purchased from the Guernsey Information Centre, Airport Information Desk, police station and from some garages and newsagents.

Cycling

(See also under Active Pursuits, page 110.) Bikes can be hired from Millard & Co, 9–11 Victoria Street, St Peter Port (tel: 01481-720 777; www.millards.org) or Guernsey Cycle Hire, North Plantation, St Peter Port (tel: 07781-192 033; www.guernseyhire.co.uk).

Cycle hire shops are plentiful on Alderney (by the harbour in Braye, and in Victoria Street) and on Sark (at the top of Harbour Hill and along The Avenue).

Inter-island ferries and France

Herm: Travel Trident (tel: 01481-721 379; www.traveltrident.com) operates ferries from St Peter Port to Herm roughly every hour in summer, with fewer boats in the off-peak season. Go early to avoid the day-trippers in the summer. The booking office is on the corner of North Esplanade and St Julian's Pier.

Sark: The Isle of Sark Shipping Company (tel: 01481-724 059; www.sark shippingcompany.com) runs day trips to Sark with five ferries a day in summer.

Rent a bicycle to best experience the island of Sark.

Alderney: the fastest, though certainly not the cheapest, way to visit the smaller island of Alderney from Guernsey is to take the 15-minute flight operated by Aurigny or Blue Islands (see page 115).

Day trips to Jersey and France: Condor Ferries (www.condorferries.co.uk) operates day trips from St Peter Port to Jersey, and to St-Malo in France. Manche Îles Express (www.manche-iles.com) operates ferries connecting Guernsey with Jersey, and Carteret, Diélette and Granville in Normandy (both take 60 minutes).

Taxis

Guernsey has licensed taxis at three ranks: in central St Peter Port, one at St Sampson's (on the bridge) and another at the airport. Pre-booking is advisable whenever possible. Taxi companies include: A+S Taxis, tel: 07781-125 544; Island Taxis, tel: 01481-700 500; 1st Call Taxis, tel: 07911-727 970; Panza Taxis, tel: 07781 111340.

FACTS FOR THE VISITOR

Disabled travellers

For information for disabled travellers in Guernsey, go to www.disabledgo.com/en/org/guernsey-1. The Radar National Key Scheme, which enables disabled people to access locked public toilets, operates in Guernsey. Visitors are advised to bring their own key; alternatively they are available from the Guernsey Information Centre.

On-street parking and public car parks have designated areas for UK and European Blue Badge holders. Guernsey buses are accessible for all

The Condor Ferry departs from St Peter Port, bound for the mainland.

wheelchairs apart from those over 29ins (75cm) wide, or a wheelchair and occupant weighing a total of more than 660lbs (300kg).

Emergencies

Dial 999 for police, fire, ambulance or coastal rescue services. The Princess Elizabeth Hospital, at Rue Mignot, St Andrews, Guernsey (tel: 01481-725 241), has a 24-hour emergency unit. There is no longer a reciprocal health agreement between Guernsey and the UK and hospital treatment is charged for, with a very limited number of exemptions. Primary care doctors and dentists are in private practice and all patients are required to pay for treatment. Comprehensive medical insurance is therefore strongly recommended.

Herm has no medical facilities, though helicopter-borne emergency services are available. Sark has a surgery opposite the Island Hall (tel: 01481-832 045, or in an emergency telephone 01481-832 045). Alderney has the small Mignot Memorial Hospital (tel: 01481-822 822) and a Medical Centre at Sundial House, Les Rocquettes (tel: 01481-822 077).

Money

Sterling is the currency of the island. Guernsey also has its own currency, in the same denominations as UK notes and coins, apart from the fact that it still has £1 notes. Both UK and Guernsey currency can be used within the islands but Channel Island sterling will not be accepted in the UK apart from in banks, which will exchange notes. Some shops will accept euros, although change will generally be given in sterling. All major debit and credit cards are widely accepted throughout the islands. ATM machines are widespread apart from on Sark and Herm, where there are none.

The Guernsey pound is legal tender on the islands only.

The lack of VAT and low duty on imported luxury items is mainly offset by the higher transport costs.

Opening times

Bank, shop and post office opening times are the same as those of the UK. Most museums and tourist attractions are open from 9am or 10am to 5pm from April to October, with some of the major sites open all year. For a list of current openings visit the Guernsey Tourism website (www.visitguernsey.com). In Guernsey pubs are normally open Monday to Saturday from 11am until late, with slightly shorter hours on a Sunday.

Telephones

Most mobiles will work on the islands but some networks require a roaming facility plus international dialling code. Pay-as-you-go phones only operate where there is an agreement with the network provider. Check with your service provider prior to departure.

The Tourist Information Centre in Guernsey will help plan your trip.

The code for Guernsey, Herm, Sark and Alderney is 01481 from the UK and +44 1481 internationally. Although the code appears to be a UK one, the Channel Islands are excluded from the UK national price rates and the costs of calls are similar to those for Europe. Most hotels offer free WiFi. Free WiFi hotspots include Guernsey Airport, the Tourist Information office and Guille-Alles Library in St Peter Port, and some cafés.

Tourist information

Guernsey Information Centre (North Esplanade, St Peter Port tel: 01481-723 552; www.visitguernsey.com) has a wealth of information on the island and can also arrange accommodation during your visit. For information on the other three islands contact:

Herm Tourism (tel: 01481-750 000; www.herm.com).

Sark Tourism, The Avenue, Sark, (tel: 01481-832 345; www.sark.com).

Alderney Tourism, 51 Victoria Street, St Anne, Alderney (tel: 01481-822 333; www.visitalderney.com).

Entertainment

To find out what's on locally, pick up a copy of The Guernsey Press or visit the Information Centre (see above)

Public phone boxes.

or their website (www.visitguernsey. com). The *St James Diary* (www.st james.gg) lists poetry readings, art exhibitions, concerts and lectures hosted by St James, the church in College Street, St Peter Port, which now forms Guernsey's premier arts venue.

Guernsey has a small, four-screen cinema showing new releases, near the airport at the Mallard Complex, La Villiaze Road, Forest (www.mallard cinema.co.uk). Alderney has a small cinema on Victoria Street, St Anne.

The Doghouse, Rohais, St Peter Port (www.doghouse.gg) is the best venue in town for live entertainment, with live music most nights, plus monthly UK tribute bands. RED (61 The Pollet, St Peter Port; www. red.gg; Mon–Sat 5pm–12.45am) has great views over the harbour and is a trendy spot for cocktails. DJs play on Fridays and Saturday evenings.

Travel documents and customs allowances

Although a passport isn't necessary for visitors arriving from the British Isles or the Republic of Ireland, airlines do require photo ID. A passport is required if you visit France.

Guernsey is not part of the EU, so you can buy duty-free goods when travelling to and from the island. Maximum allowances are 200 cigarettes or 100 cigarillos or 50 cigars or 250 grams of tobacco; 4 litres of still table wine or 8 litres if no spirits, liqueurs, fortified or sparkling wines are purchased 1 litre of spirits or strong liqueurs over 22 percent volume or two litres of fortified wine, sparkling wine or other liqueurs under 22 percent volume; 50 litres of beer or cider; £390-worth of other goods including perfume, jewellery and gifts.

Live entertainment sometimes spills onto the streets in St Peter Port.

Accommodation

From simple B&Bs to stylishly converted farmhouses and chic boutique hotels, Guernsey offers accommodation to cater for most tastes.

Accommodation is plentiful but you won't find many bargains, especially if you book your hotel independently of transport. The best deals are the packages which include air or sea transport. Many of the hotels offer this option on their websites; alternatively you can do it through specialist operators. For example, Island Getaways (tel: 0198-721 111; www.islandget aways.co.uk) offer spring deals whereby the total cost for a week's holiday in a 3- or 4-star hotel, travel included (and sometimes car hire too if you pay in advance) can work out a good deal less than the cost of accommodation alone booked through the hotel. Rates are almost invariably cheaper off-season and there are some great deals at the hotels that remain open in winter. For rooms in July and August book well ahead. Supplements are usually charged for seaview rooms; it's often worth the extra per night for the fabulous view you wake up to.

The Guernsey Tourist Board brochure (available online at www.visit guernsey.com) has a comprehensive illustrated section on accommodation available on the islands of Guernsey, Herm, Sark and Alderney. The website will also give you the latest tour operator deals. Tour companies specialising in Guernsey include Premier Holidays (tel: 0844-493 7529; www.premier holidays.co.uk/guernsey), Channel Islands' Direct (tel: 0800-640 9058; www.channelislandsdirect.co.uk) and Guernsey Travel (tel: 01534-496 660); www.guernseytravel.com)

St Peter Port offers the best sightseeing, shopping and choice of restaurants. Buses from here will take you all over the island; it is also convenient for hopping across to Herm or Sark. Alternatively there are at-

The Braye Beach Hotel offers excellent views over the sands.

tractive beach hotels, and converted farmhouses and manor houses inland.

Old-fashioned values are still often adhered to, but that doesn't mean you won't get WiFi or power showers in the upper bracket hotels. Guernsey now has its first 5-star hotel, the Old Government House Hotel & Spa, and many of the 4-stars have undergone stylish revamps in the last few years.

Most places will require credit card details before confirming a reservation, and for special deals you may need to pay in full prior to arrival. VAT is not chargeable in the Channel Islands.

Hotels, self catering and camping

The price bands below are a guideline for the cost of a standard double room and breakfast for two in high season.

£££ = over £220
££ = £120–220
£ = under £120

GUERNSEY
Bella Luce Hotel

La Fosse, St Martin, tel: 01481-238 764; www.bellalucehotel.com.

This ancient manor house has been transformed into a luxury boutique hotel, one of the most desirable on the island. It offers opulent guest rooms, some with four-poster beds, a candlelit-restaurant with top quality cuisine, a bistro, pool and spa. ££

Best Western Hotel de Havelet

Havelet, St Peter Port; tel: 01481-722 199; www.dehaveletguernsey.com.

Georgian house on a hill with fine views of the harbour and islands. It is a 15-minute walk uphill from the centre of St Peter Port – or you can take the courtesy minibus which links the hotel and town centre several times a day in summer. Indoor pool with sauna, steam room and jacuzzi. ££

Le Pollet, Guernsey's cobbled shopping street.

Cobo Bay Hotel

Cobo Coast Road, tel: 01481-257 102; www.cobobayhotel.com.

Ideal beach holiday hotel with excellent value rooms opposite sandy Cobo Bay. Award-winning restaurant. Small complimentary health suite. ££

Duke of Richmond Hotel

Cambridge Park, St Peter Port, tel: 01481-726 221; www.dukeofrichmond.com.

This comfy 4-star hotel beside Candie Gardens has a contemporary look with a black and white lounge and a Leopard Bar/Restaurant with bold stripes and 'leopardskin' fabrics. Guest room prices vary substantially depending on the degree of luxury (there's a Penthouse and three Junior suites) and the views – many overlook the sea. ££–£££

The Farmhouse

Route des Bas Courtils, St Saviour, tel: 01481-264 181; www.thefarmhouse.gg.

Run by the Nussbaumer family for three generations, this converted farmhouse is among Guernsey's favourite hotels. The 14 bedrooms are furnished in contemporary style, with large walk-in showers. Popular restaurant with meals available by the fire, poolside or in one of the gazebos. ££

Fauxquets Valley Campsite

Candie Road, Castel, tel: 01481-255 460; www.fauxquets.co.uk.

Wonderful campsite in a tranquil valley. All amenities including heated pool, licensed restaurant and bar, shop and children's playground and games room. Open May–August. £

Fleur du Jardin

Kings Mills, Castel, tel: 01481-257 996; www.fleurdujardin.com.

Named after a breed of Guernsey cow, this old farmhouse has been stylishly renovated and offers rooms with bleached timber walls and sandstone

La Frégate Hotel.

bathrooms. First-class gastro-pub food, solar-heated pool and, from May to August, a health suite. ££

Hotel La Michele

Les Hubits, St Martins, tel: 01481-239 492; www.lamichelehotel.com.

This small family-run hotel, with 16 ensuite rooms, is renowned for hospitality. Restaurant, bar and attractive heated outdoor swimming pool in secluded gardens. £

La Frégate Hotel

Les Cotils, St Peter Port, tel: 01481-724 624; www.lafregatehotel.com.

Stylish, deluxe boutique hotel in its own grounds in St Peter Port. Fantastic views across the islands and arguably the best restaurant in Guernsey (see page 29). £££

La Rochelle Guest House

Rohais de Haut, Castel, tel: 01481-258 088; www.larocheguesthouseguernsey.com.

One of Guernsey's loveliest guest houses: a charming Georgian home in peaceful grounds in the centre of the island. The hospitable owners are also excellent cooks, providing copious breakfasts and evening meals on request. £

Mille Fleurs Self Catering

Rue du Bordage, St Pierre du Bois, tel: 01481-263 911; www.millefleurs.co.uk.

Comfortable self-catering cottages set in a peaceful rural location with internationally acclaimed gardens. Heated outdoor swimming pool. Open all year. £870–2,150 per week depending on size and season. £–££

The Old Government House Hotel & Spa

St Ann's Place, St Peter Port, tel: 01481-724 921; www.theoghhotel.com.

The former official residence of Guernsey's governor, the OGH (as it's familiarly known) dates from 1858 and has recently been extensively refurbished and upgraded. This is the

When booking at the White House Hotel, ask for a room with a sea view.

only five-star hotel on the island. Expect plush bedrooms, top-notch cuisine in the Brasserie or Curry Room, traditional afternoon teas and excellent service. Leisure facilities include a health club, Moroccan-style spa and outdoor heated pool. £££

St Pierre Park Hotel
Rohais, St Peter Port; tel: 01481-728 282; www.handpickedhotels.co.uk.
Luxurious but slightly impersonal modern hotel set in 35 acres of parkland on the outskirts of St Peter Port. Ideal for sports enthusiasts with a 9-hole golf course, tennis courts, indoor pool and newly refurbished health club and spa. Eating options include the excellent Pavilion Brasserie, with an emphasis on fresh Guernsey produce. Good value for a 4-star hotel. ££

Ziggurat
5 Constitution Steps, St Peter Port, tel: 01481-723 008; www.hotelzigg urat.com.
Bucking the trend of traditional island hotels is the new Moroccan-inspired Ziggurat, just above the old quarter with fine views over St Peter Port harbour. This boutique hotel has 14 en-suite rooms and a restaurant serving Merguez sausage, tagines and tabouleh. ££

HERM

White House Hotel
Herm, GY1 3HR, tel: 01481-750 075; www.herm.com.
Ideal place to unwind away from the 21st century. Family run for over half a century with old-fashioned values, good service and excellent food and wine. Swimming pool, tennis court and croquet lawn. Holiday cottages and a campsite with sea-facing terraces are also available. £££

SARK

La Sablonnerie
Sark, tel: 01481-832 061; www.lasa blonnerie.com.
A total escape – located on Little Sark, this remote farmhouse hotel is reached by the owner's horse-drawn

carriages and offers rural tranquillity, plus excellent cuisine and comfortable rooms. One of the loveliest hotels on the Channel Islands. £££

Stocks Hotel

Sark, tel: 01481-832 001; www.stocks hotel.com.

This lovely country house in a wooded valley leading to Dixcart Bay has very comfy, individually-designed guest rooms and an excellent restaurant (see page 93). £££

ALDERNEY

The Adventurer's Rest

St Anne, tel: 01481-824 784; www. adventurersrest.co.uk.

This new hotel opened in 2016 in the heart of St Anne, with 20 ensuite rooms, bar and restaurant and sunny terrace for meals or cream teas. £

Braye Beach Hotel

Braye Street; tel: 01481-824 300; www.brayebeach.com.

Chic designer hotel with a perfect setting overlooking Braye Beach. All rooms have bathrobes, a complimentary decanter of sherry and free WiFi. Book ahead for sea-view rooms. For the restaurant, see page 105. ££–£££

Farm Court

Le Petit Val, Alderney, tel: 01481-822 075; www.farmcourt-alderney.co.uk.

B&B in small converted barns with generous breakfasts, plus an owner who gives painting lessons. Self-catering also available. Good value for money. £

Fort Clonque

Contact The Landmark Trust, Shottesbrooke, Maidenhead, Berkshire, SL6 3SW, tel: 01628-825 925; www.landmarktrust.org.uk.

Built in the 1840s, Fort Clonque is cut off from Alderney at high tide, so suits those with a sense of adventure. The fort has been converted to surprisingly comfortable self-catering accommodation, with sleeping quarters for up to 13 people (or 14 if you count the ghost) and spectacular views. Four nights from £768.

La Sablonnerie hotel uses produce from its farm and gardens.

Index

Credits

Insight Guides Great Breaks Guernsey
Editor: Sarah Clark
Author: Susie Boulton
Head of Production: Rebeka Davies
Picture Editor: Tom Smyth
Cartography Update: Carte
Photo credits: Caragh Chocolates 92T;
Dreamstime 109B; Getty Images 4/5, 74T;
Guernsey Press 53B; iStock 103T; La Frigate
124; Mockford & Bonetti/Apa Publications
6MC, 6ML, 7M, 7TR, 7M, 8/9, 9, 10, 11T,
12T, 12B, 14, 16T, 16B, 17B, 17T, 18T, 18B,
19T, 20, 21T, 21B, 22T, 22B, 23T, 23B, 26T,
26B, 27, 28T, 32, 33, 34, 35T, 35B, 36, 37T,
38B, 39, 40, 44T, 46B, 46T, 47B, 47T, 49,
50TL, 51, 52, 53T, 54, 55, 56T, 57B, 57T, 59T,
58B, 60T, 60B, 61, 62, 64T, 64B, 65, 66T, 66B,
67T, 68T, 68B, 69B, 69T, 72, 73, 75T, 75B, 77T,
78, 80ML, 81T, 82, 83, 84T, 84B, 85B, 87T,
87B, 89, 90T, 92B, 94, 95, 97B, 98, 99B, 100B,
101T, 101B, 102B, 102T, 103B, 104T, 108,
109T, 110B, 111, 112, 117, 118, 119, 120B,
123; Visit Guernsey 6ML, 6MR, 7T, 7MR, 7BR,
11B, 13, 19B, 25T, 24B, 25, 28B, 31, 31T,
31B, 37B, 38T, 41, 42, 43, 44B, 45, 48, 50ML,
50/51T, 56B, 59, 67B, 70T, 70B, 74B, 76B, 77,
79, 80TL, 85T, 86, 88T, 88B, 90B, 91T, 91B,
93, 96B, 96T, 97T, 99T, 100T, 104B, 106/107,
110T, 113B, 113T, 114, 115, 116, 120T, 121,
122, 125, 126
Cover credits: iStock (main) Shutterstock
(BL&BR)

CONTACT US:
Every effort has been made to provide
accurate information in this publication,
but changes are inevitable. The publisher
cannot be responsible for any resulting loss,
inconvenience or injury. We would appreciate
it if readers would call our attention to any
errors or outdated information. We also
welcome your suggestions; please contact us
at: hello@insightguides.com

All Rights Reserved
© 2017 Apa Digital (CH) AG and
Apa Publications (UK) Ltd

Third Edition 2017

Printed in China by CTPS

Distribution
UK, Ireland and Europe: Apa Publications
(UK) Ltd; sales@insightguides.com
United States and Canada: Ingram Publisher
Services; ips@ingramcontent.com
Australia and New Zealand: Woodslane;
info@woodslane.com.au
Southeast Asia: Apa Publications (SN) Pte;
singaporeoffice@insightguides.com
Hong Kong, Taiwan and China:
Apa Publications (HK) Ltd;
hongkongoffice@insightguides.com
Worldwide: Apa Publications (UK) Ltd;
sales@insightguides.com
**Special Sales, Content Licensing and
CoPublishing**
Insight Guides can be purchased in bulk
quantities at discounted prices. We can
create special editions, personalised
jackets and corporate imprints tailored
to your needs. sales@insightguides.com;
www.insightguides.biz